IT'S MY TURN
...Now, Where Was I ?

Kathy,

Dreams do come true.
Mine did. Enjoy.

Julie Fairfield Felicelli
2007

Julie Fairfield Felicelli
Illustrated by David Messing

First Page Publications

For more information
or to reorder
please visit
www.mamafel.com

Summary: The funny and whimsical observations of life as a mother, woman, and human are chronicled.

ISBN # 1-928623-80-8
I. Felicelli, Julie Fairfield. II. Title
Library of Congress Control Number: 2005936688

Dedication

To my husband, Joe, who came home each night when he knew there would be chaos, who smiled when he could have run screaming into the night, who understood my need to be creative beyond giving birth, who hurdled laundry piles and dodged flying toys with much grace, who tried valiantly to guide me towards organization and show me the merits of a tidy household, and who was such a good sport when he threw in the towel after thirty-three years and hired a team of housekeepers.

With clean bathrooms, a dust–free environment and vacuumed floors, my guilt at never catching up dissolved and there it was—time for me to pursue my dream. I so appreciate his support, excitement, and encouraging nudges as I step beyond my comfort zone. I thank God every day for my good fortune in choosing him as my first and only life partner. He might have had something totally different in mind when he said, "I do," but thirty-five years later, I think it's safe to say that he has earned an A for effort, and more importantly, for perseverance.

Acknowledgment

Life on this planet only makes sense if we look around and appreciate the simplicity, beauty, and humans around us. The absolute joy of my life has been my association with the people I call family and the friends I have encountered in our many moves over the last several decades. I can measure my happiness in the amount of laughter generated from these people, and if that is the gauge, I am one happy individual.

To my family: Joe, Jennifer, Joseph, Emily, Mark, Annie, Julie Jr., and Daniel, whose activities and behavior supplied most of the material herein, who designed my business cards, set-up my website, mailed notices, and believed that I could actually write this book.

To Dr. Sue Anderson, whose talent and dedication to chiropractic and NAET helped me get to a healthier place in my life so I had the energy and stamina to accomplish my dream.

To my relatives and friends all over the country, who were relentless through the years, telling me that I should believe in myself.

To Pam Grisby, who brought me the brochure on how to get published at the perfect time in my life. To Jennifer Simich, who challenged me when I questioned my abilities and talent.

To Tina Kohlfeld, whose photographic talents are so appreciated for my picture on the biography page.

To the entire staff at First Page Publications: Marian, who said, "Let's do this," and Katherine, my editor, who promised to keep the passion, and to Sarah, Liz, Kim, and Joe, who field my phone calls and answer my pesky and absurd questions without tearing out their hair.

To Dave Messing, whose artistic genius brought spirit and life to my dream. I especially thank him for giving my character better looking legs than I actually possess.

The Perfect Union . . .
As Unions Go

Honeymoon Hotel

What was your honeymoon experience? Do you have pictures of breathtaking scenes in an exotic wonderland, the two of you basking in the romance that dreams are made of? Do the two of you look like the luckiest, happiest people in the world? Do me a favor and send me a copy of *your* pictures, please. I'll put them in my album and pretend they belong to us.

Our wedding was great. It was a simple affair that didn't make the papers. More people than we invited came to celebrate our union. Cute, little Slovakian women cooked their hearts out and catered to our Italian souls. Learning that my husband was a chocolate lover, they designed the top cake layer in chocolate so he would be happy and surprised at our first anniversary celebration. Everyone danced, there were no ugly scenes, and off we drove to begin our life together.

A real honeymoon would have to wait. My groom was in graduate school and just two days after the wedding would take final exams for his summer courses. No big deal. We'd have time later. The important thing was that I had found a good man. We would enjoy a good life with not too many roller coaster moments. Our first night together would be at a Chicago hotel and we would head for our Indiana home in the morning. Now you might be thinking of the Drake or the Palmer House but we were on an extremely tight budget, so dash those thoughts from your mind. We were young and in love enough to know the place was not important. We were a Mr. and Mrs. and that was all that mattered. And then we pulled up to the front door of our hotel in the heart of the Windy City. Well, maybe not the heart. It was more like the pancreas, maybe the kidney. We couldn't tell if it was valet service or a vandal hoping to steal our car. We played it safe and parked ourselves. Out I jumped, clutching my purse to my chest in my white, two-piece suit with gold buttons. My father had pinned an orchid corsage on me as we left. I made a mental note to use the corsage pin to defend myself, if necessary. We registered as Mr. and Mrs. and we got the look from the desk clerk like, "Sure you are, and my name is Mister Magoo. Listen, we don't care what your story is. Just go to your room and don't break anything."

We got in the elevator with four other couples who were quite anxious to get to their rooms on the same floor as ours. I guess we didn't go fast enough as some of them began to lick each other and unbutton portions of their clothing. We leapt through the elevator doors, opened the door to our room, locked it quickly and breathed a sigh of relief that we had survived so far. This would be the night we had waited for. A few things to take care of and the night would be ours. It was essential to check to see if the

Chicago White Sox were playing on TV. No Sox, we checked the Cubs channel. It was years before cable so we only had to check three or four channels for the groom to assure himself that he would not be missing anything important in the sports world. As we unpacked, we heard a knock. We responded through the locked door and the intruder explained, "Uh, were there any clothes or suitcases in the room when you entered? It seems we gave keys for the same room to two different parties and it might be necessary to move you." We assured them there was nothing in the room before we got there and then proceeded to push all the furniture we could move in front of the door, just in case. No one was going to interrupt the night we had waited for, the night we had dreamt of for so many years. I slipped into the bathroom to change into the special nightgown my sisters had given me for my shower. I had noticed flannel pajamas on the edge of the bed and prayed his mother had packed them in case the hotel was over air-conditioned. August, Chicago, and flannel should never be used in the same sentence. It didn't matter. It was our first night together, the beginning of many wonderful nights. I came out of the bathroom and accepted the outreached hand of my flannel-pajama-clad husband. "Shall we?" he asked and I nodded. As we moved toward the bed, now pushed up against the door, he looked at me with those blue eyes that made me melt. "Are you sure you're ready for this?" he asked, stroking my shoulder. "I've never been more ready for anything in my life," I uttered breathlessly. One more check to make sure the door was secured to ensure our total privacy. He sat me down on the bed, reached for the covers and pulled them back. And then it happened. He reached under the bed and pulled out my overnight bag. We spent the next hour doing what couples dream of. Who could have guessed we'd get that many gift envelopes? "Boy, we must be rich," both of us said together. We threw money and checks into the air, twirling and jumping up and down on the bed in unadulterated excitement. Exhausted, we fell asleep happy in each other's arms, clutching our wealth tightly. We were still leery about the key thing and didn't want to take any chances. It was the perfect start to a union that would last forever or at least until the money ran out. We never did take a honeymoon, but how could you top a night like that? I guess we don't need your picture-perfect photos after all. The hotel was kind enough to send us the surveillance video from the elevator and of us jumping on the bed.

The Great White Hunter

There are some lightbulb moments that can have a lasting impression on someone you love and we came up with the mother of all ideas that knocked the socks off any thoughts my husband might have about entering the mid-life-crisis arena. I was one of the younger moms in every group I joined, so it gave me a wonderful chance to watch and learn something about life and relationships. The news was not good. Most of the talk centered on husbands and the "weird" things they were doing. It seemed they were experiencing mid-life crises, causing them to get perms, buy sport cars or, in more drastic cases, take off with their nubile secretaries. It was something to consider since I would be there in a few years myself. Taking a good look at couples, I realized that these baby boomer men were, in some instances, raised their first few years by moms and grandparents while their fathers served in the war, or were born shortly after their fathers returned. Dads were tough men who had little time for outward signs of affection. The lines were drawn in ink: men worked and provided for their families and women did the rest. There would always be a time to fulfill dreams after retirement.

For now, *keep your head down, nose to the grindstone and don't ask questions* seemed to be the rule of thumb. Enter the women's movement.

As much as it was a blessing for women to be recognized as a power source in this masculine world, it left many men scrambling, scratching their heads in utter befuddlement. As we know, men aren't poster children for the "Change Is Good" theory and many dug in their heels rather than jump on board the *times they are-a changin'* train. In our case, I noticed that our head of household took nothing for himself and if he did have time to take inventory, would see that everything he earned was used as fast as he made it. Our seventh child was not on the horizon yet, but the first six were in middle school and high school and their needs took the checkbook to a zero balance on a regular basis. How could I avoid his impending crisis, this man who still had the shoes he wore at our wedding eighteen years earlier? Telling him that only Santa's elves wore shoes that curled at the toes, we had to hog tie him and drag him to the shoe store to pick another pair. I think he still holds the Guinness World's Record for most half soles and heels on one pair of shoes. We've invested more in that one pair of shoes than we paid for our first car. Anyhow, we had to avert the crisis which we knew was already somewhere on the radar screen. Maybe he could have his dream early. Why wait for retirement and be too old to physically handle it or God forbid, forget why he even wanted to do it?

For years he had expressed the desire to go on a photographic safari to Kenya. Another dream was to take a hot air balloon trip. My mind had barely begun the creative process when the answer presented itself, via the U.S. Postal Service. The Brookfield Zoo in Chicago sent a brochure offering an eighteen-day photographic safari to Kenya (hooray) with the option of a hot air balloon trip over a game preserve (yipee). A quick call to get information and my reservation check was in the afternoon mail. A three-hundred-dollar deposit would hold his place while we tried to convince him to take the opportunity and run with it. It would not be easy. We were expecting a small bonus check in the next week and it would be used for the usual — fix the garage, repair the roof — with nothing for him to mark the occasion. Not this year, we decided. The whole bonus check would pay for the trip with a little spending money and there would be no discussion about it.

To carry out our plan, we went to the local bookstore and bought maps of Kenya and laid them around the house. In the bathroom near the throne we opened the encyclopedia to the section on Kenya where we knew he would be a captive audience, for at least a short time. I had purchased giant wicker bugs (don't ask why) some years earlier and attached them now to the drapes along with gauze swags to make it look like a jungle atmosphere. The purchase of a photojournalist's vest with twenty-something pockets for film, and the gift of a bwana hat from his boss finished off our scheme and he still resisted. "I can't take that kind of time off," he lamented. Like the whole company would go belly up while he was gone. "You have to come with me" he insisted. It wasn't my dream. If he wanted to hang out in the savannah in his underwear, it should be his choice. Eat when he wanted to, sleep when he wanted to; we would pay the extra for him to have private accommodations. His underwear was another vestige from our wedding day, so his privacy was in the best interests of the tour group. "We can't afford it" was his last attempt to maintain his bleak existence but it fell on deaf ears. The bonus check would be used for the purpose for which it was intended. It was intended as a "thank you" for *his* hard work. Curiosity finally won him over and we noticed an amazing difference. He came home from work regularly at a decent hour and pored over the information strewn about the house for his perusal. We knew he was hooked when he made no fuss about the malaria and typhoid shots he would get, and he even bought himself a new camera and fifty rolls of film for the trip. He got into the plan phase with a vengeance and a new man emerged, happy and with a purpose.

The whole family loaded into the car to drop him off at the airport on the scheduled day and we waved goodbye, crossing our fingers that he would have a fabulous time on what we would forever call his "Pre-Mid-Life Crisis Extravaganza." He would return ecstatic from his experience. Our pain would come upon his return, though, as we sat through more than our share of slide presentations, showcasing the 840 pictures he took on the trip. We weaned them down to a poignant 380, explaining that forty-six shots of the same wildebeest squatting for a personal moment weren't as interesting as he might think. His excuse was that he was trying to show desert, grassland, and marsh land-scape all in the same picture. The wildebeest must have wandered into the lens frame out of desperation.

It's been almost seventeen years since the trip and the two chairs, screen, and slide carousels are still set up in the basement, ready to go at a moment's notice. Unsuspecting visitors never know what hit them until it's too late. We use it as a bad behavior deterrent to this day on the kids. The threat of having to sit through one more showing of the slides has a miraculous effect on sibling squabbles. One mention of the punishment available and it's a *Leave It To Beaver* moment that would have made June and Ward Cleaver proud. But our safari tourist was forever changed by that trip. It gave him something to brag about at the water cooler. The good news is that even now, if he whines about any little thing, we remind him that he has already experienced his top two dreams and we send him down to the punishment area to refresh his memory. It's like a B-12 shot and he always emerges with a look of satisfaction and accomplishment. It's so rewarding for him and us when he responds to someone who asks if he's been anywhere. If you're anywhere near the house, though, be prepared for the jihad of slide shows. He has purchased a laser pointer and will even put on the vest and hat if you appreciate ambience. Oh, and if you ever want to get out of our house, whatever you do, don't ask if he took the wildlife pictures all over the walls. If you're here long enough, you may be escorted to the guest room, which we all know as "The Safari Room." It'll be too late for you by then. No one escapes unscathed from "The Safari Room." I knew I'd need those wicker bugs someday. They're hanging from the bed posts. Watching you . . .

Crime Scene

We've been robbed! Or at least ransacked. From the top of the stairs it is inevitable that the first floor has been the target of someone's anger, madness, or a combination of the two. Absolutely everything is out of place, worse than usual. We're not known for a museum-like home but this is a travesty. Lamps are down, shades crushed, papers from the desk all over, table legs broken, furniture overturned. Who would do this? What did they hope to find? The only thing left in its original place, ironically, is the motto I embroidered and framed back in the '70s to sum up our household condition: *Never Clean, Always Open*. In shock, I stumble through the mess to try to get a handle on what happened here. I race to the one area where our valuables are kept and they have not been touched. Our autographed Walter Payton, Dick Butkus, and Gale Sayers footballs are still in their cases and my treasured Meadowlark Lemon basketball is still on the shelf, nestled in its silver tray. They weren't after our treasures. What, then?

Sifting through the mess, I find it hard to gather my thoughts. The devastation is total and I consider calling the police to report the incident. Maybe there's a nasty bunch of vandals whose parents believe they are lighting candles at church when they are actually committing crimes around the neighborhood, and I make a mental note not to touch anything more in case there are finger-prints. The phone has to be here somewhere. And then I see it. All the evidence I need to know who was here and exactly what happened. There will be no need to call the authorities. Across the room, in the small alcove where the telephone table, lamp, and Ukrainian egg collection used to be is the weapon used in this diabolical disaster. And the body is nearby, on its back where it fell. I am no longer surprised, and buried memories begin to emerge, faintly at first, then all too clearly. The house could look worse. It has happened before and, unfortunately, will happen many more times unless we can stop this act of unadulterated insanity.

We did have a perpetrator in our home after I went to bed last night. It wasn't a neighborhood vandal or a crazed bandit. It was, instead, a common, ordinary, little housefly who had the misfortune of coming through an open door. My husband, armed with his rolled up newspaper, was determined to save us all from the mortal dangers we all know flies present. In Rambo fashion he tracked it down, room to room, chasing it up and down the hall and into windows repeatedly, knocking over everything in his and the fly's path. In the past, we have seen exhausted flies just lie down to await their fate rather than take another moment of the unleashed fury around them. Some have received whiplash injuries from the air currents the flailing newspaper caused and just pretended to be dead. He's not fooled for a minute. Even with their little legs up and gossamer wings perfectly still, he has been known to wonk them hard enough to flip them up, over and back again. He can be heard roaring, while wielding his paper saber, "No fly shall live in this house while I'm Lord and Master." There's sure not much left of his kingdom when he's through, though. Even the Salvation Army doesn't return our calls when we leave messages for a pickup. I overheard something in the background about not having enough glue for repairs of that magnitude.

I'll clean up the mess. I'll bury the poor creature with his kinfolk in the back yard, wrapped in what's left of the matted, rolled-up newspaper. I sometimes leave the little body out for viewing for a short time as a deterrent to his relatives. "It's not a pretty sight in here. Don't let this happen to you," I sing out into the airwaves, hoping all flying insects hear me. I try to tell my husband that if he's not going to escort them peacefully from the house, he has to find some nondestructive alternatives. It's all in the wrist; it's a game of patience. If you're lucky, they tire themselves out and make easy targets. They are so busy panting, they don't hear the fly swatter approaching. Or, after listening to our *Phantom of the Opera* CD six times in a row, they are too happy to fly out as soon as the door opens. My husband just mumbled something about remaining proactive and I wouldn't understand. I think he muttered something like, "War is war, after all."

I stopped newspaper delivery to limit his choice of weapons. Then I found a desecrated *Smithsonian* under our bed, wrapped around a can of *Black Flag*. He's calling in the big guns now. I just pray that there's a little *Fly Gazette* or something so the word will get out for all things that fly to avoid our home. It's better for everyone involved, and especially our furniture. I paid for materials to be sent to our home so he could read about the avoidance of fly hostilities but I caught him rolling up the pamphlets, heading for another hapless flying victim. It's no use. If it's not too late, I'll send for an application for one of the kids to get into the carpenter apprentice program. It's my only hope. I'm running out of furniture.

The Affair

I t was bound to happen. My husband is having an affair. Yes, the divorce rate is at an all-time high and marital infidelity is beyond outrageous, but I never thought it would happen here in my realm. With our 35th anniversary on the horizon, I thought we had passed all the danger zones. We sailed past the Seven Year Itch, and literally somersaulted over the ten-year speed bump. We had six kids by then and there was little time to think about anything but laundry, meals, attacks of head lice, who looked at who the wrong way, or who got the most M&Ms. We were too exhausted to have extramarital thoughts, let alone act on them. The twenty-year mark brought us to the realization that in another decade most of them would be out of college and we might have a chance at peace. For two decades, we waved at each other as we passed in hallways during the madness of teacher conferences and even from separate cars at intersections as we hurried to get the kids to their music lessons or sports games. At thirty years, we were giddy in the knowledge that our marital pact was still intact: Whoever decides to leave the union gets immediate possession of all the children until death do they part. It was a fabulous deterrent and worked marvelously . . . until now.

I should have seen it coming. The extra errands, asking to do a few of my more unpleasant tasks "to help me out," spending an unusual amount of time cruising in the car. He was actually inventing ways to leave the house, his haven! I was suspicious but never once did I believe it could be anything serious. I was so wrong.

To get to the bottom of things, I asked to accompany him on one of his "errands." He fidgeted at first, squirmed a little, but when he saw the look in my eye, he knew the jig was up. He agreed, ready to confess and willing to let me meet her. It was worse than I could have imagined. We got in the car. He adjusted the mirrors, put in some suspiciously sultry CDs, and buckled up. I strapped on my seat belt and prepared myself for the jolt. He ran his hands through his hair and then the transformation began. He passed his hand wistfully over the GPS (global positioning system), caressing the dial. With a gentle twist, he engaged the system and that's when I knew the enemy was before me. "User One," the provocative voice intoned. "Destination," she continued. "Calculating route," she purred. I was no match for this vixen. She had all the answers. We were heading to the dry cleaners, only a few miles away, but he listened to her every command as if in a trance. "Bear to the right in point five miles," brought him to attention and he waited with bated breath for the Pavlovian bell signal that would give him license to obey. "Left turn in point two miles," she spoke as if draped in a negligee, sliding across a credenza. He was mesmerized by her voice and it was apparent he was ready, willing and able to comply with her every wish. I sure didn't get that response a few weeks ago when I mentioned that he might take a look at the waterfall leaking through the ceiling under the laundry room. No, this was more complicated than I was prepared for. On the short drive home he went around the circle in the cul de sac a few more times than necessary, just to hear her say, "you have arrived," and I swear the look on his face indicated that he was mentally lighting an afterglow cigarette! I got out, bewildered, and he lingered, pretending to readjust the seat and mirrors. More likely he wanted to apologize for the last minute intrusion on my part.

The next day we took a prearranged trip to return our granddaughters to their mother and he actually suggested taking his car, as if more familiarity with the temptress would make me understand his plight. I only half listened to their touchy-feely conversation as I prepared the girls and myself for the three-hour ride. Our personal conversations were interrupted continually with her five mile, two mile, point five mile warnings and the inevitable bell, signaling the call to execute the appropriate maneuver. At one point he handed me a map to check the route (a consolation gesture, perhaps?), and I noted that we could take a shortcut and save ourselves twenty miles and at least that many minutes. His struggle was total as he weighed his two options. My heart sank as he stayed the course and followed her directions blindly through a small town with more intersections and lights than the Las Vegas Strip, most of them red for our entertainment.

He appeared sheepish when we came to the intersection where we could have been ages ago had we taken the shortcut, but there was no apology from him, or her, for that matter. Her hold over him deepened as she chided him to make a safe U-turn at his earliest convenience when we exited for gas. Rather inflexible of her, I thought. She caught herself and returned to her "Recalculating Route" mode to secure his trust anew. By the time we pulled back into our driveway, I leapt out of the vehicle, eager to be in the house. Complaints and whining were actually more reassuring sounds than the drone of her voice, always in command.

My chance to test her further came the next day when my husband took an unexpected trip out of the country. Afraid she would be stolen from the airport parking lot, he left her in the study and I lost no time installing her in my car. I pretended I was him, *User One*, but she was not fooled for a minute. She would not allow me to type in my destination, would not calculate the route, and went, instead, to the *here's the route you are taking and I could care less where it takes you or how long.* I pressed every button, demanding that she respond to my simple request (a trip to the nearby Wal-Mart) but she silently refused to engage or even acknowledge my existence. Stubbornly, I continued to press buttons, taunting her to respond, to get mad, to show her temper, to give me the satisfaction of hearing her annoyance. And that's when it happened. Her aggravating silence was replaced by a soothing, personable male voice (did I detect a Spanish accent?) who gently supplied me with the information to find my way to Wal-Mart and suggested the shortest route, for my added pleasure. He couldn't have been more helpful. From Wal-Mart, I was guided gently to the sewing machine repair shop, the grocery store, the gas station, and finally towards home. I felt the emotional hug as he announced my arrival. As I slid from the car I couldn't help myself; I turned back, unable to say goodbye. With a flip of the switch we were together again. We had developed a bond, a trust. Could I leave him alone in the cold garage? He deserved much better. I slid my scarf from my neck and gently draped it around him, reassuring him that I would be back very soon. Shakespeare was right: parting IS such sweet sorrow. Until then, Fernando . . .

Rhythm

Rhythm is tricky in more ways than its spelling. I was so proud in the fourth grade when I was the only one who remembered that the "*h*" came before the "*y*" and spelled it correctly. In music class, we clapped and pounded the table learning rhythm and I heard the word mentioned again when grown-ups talked about it and then they'd laugh about how many kids they had. It wasn't until years later that I ever really understood anything about the big deal concerning rhythm or, more particularly, the rhythm method. It seemed to involve a whole lot of paying attention to the body's processes, fluids and other yucky stuff and the desire for that amount of detail always eluded me. I was satisfied that I possessed *rhythm* and there was a *method* to my madness but the two together . . . I don't think so.

Once married, rhythm took on a whole new meaning. I did have a sort of rhythm thing going, I guess. It seemed I was the proud owner of two seasons of birthing, late spring and late fall. If it was spring, I was bound to give birth to girls; in the late fall, boys. And, in a sort of weird rhythm, I had a girl, then a boy, then a girl, then a boy, then a girl, then a boy. So it was spring, fall, spring, fall, spring, fall as far as my seasons of delivery. I'm sure I didn't break any records or gain entry into the Guinness Book of World Records, but it intrigued me enough to pay attention after the first three were born. I never took precautions but I was careful to be personally unavailable in both January and August. It wasn't easy since all of the girls were born approximately nine months after our anniversary in August (the gift that kept on giving) and the boys were all born approximately nine months and a week after the Super Bowl. Apparently distraught that there were no games to watch and his hobbies nonexistent beyond sports, I was a natural fallback. It was an ongoing science project, and after six births, it was safe to say we would have had dozens before it was over if we didn't find a less productive way to spend our time.

Mother Nature has a way of stepping in and she came to my rescue by afflicting me with a raging estrogen blitz. At thirty, my health took a dive. No one wanted to come near me, not even me, for the next ten years. Doctors would insist it was all in my mind and prescribe pills. Not to cure me, mind you. The pills would send me to a happy place where everything looked peaceful, orderly and under control. And while I was there, the kids put the house on the market and took power of attorney. It wasn't a pretty sight. Finally, an insightful doctor recognized that there was actually a physical condition present and with a small adjustment in hormones, I was as good as new, more or less. Nine months and three weeks after the Super Bowl, the baby was born and indeed it was a boy. I guess I do have some kind of rhythm. I tried to donate my body to science so they could investigate and save others from the effects of advanced rhythm-itis. My application was returned with a big, red REJECTED on it. The cover letter said that my uterus had too much mileage on it to be of any use. Imagine that. That same hormone problem has returned. I have decided not to get it repaired and to live with it until menopause saves me. The next baby would be a girl if my rhythm pattern holds and I think you'd agree with me. Four girls with excellent memories, some of them prenatal, are more than enough for any mother — especially this mother. It's no picnic to be reminded of your shortcomings, especially before they were born. But just to be sure, we sign their father up for out-of-the-country business trips in January and August. There's nothing wrong with his rhythm. It's his memory I worry about. Just last week, he said it would be great if all the kids came back home to live. Bursting into tears probably wasn't the reaction he was hoping for. He'll think it's my hormone problem. It'll be our little secret.

Duck Day

E ach year our family celebrates March 13th. It's not anybody's birthday, not our anniversary, nothing special to anyone but us—actually, anyone but me and my friend Pam's husband, Greg. We were forever changed on that day in 2002.

It started out like any other winter Monday in Michigan, cold but sunny. The snow had melted and the hope of spring loomed. Our granddaughter, Tai, had come to stay with us and she got up extra early to say goodbye to each family member as they left for work or school. Scraping up last evening's activities from the family room floor, I heard pleasantries exchanged from uncle to niece and then the door slammed, and there was a moment of welcomed silence. Hearing a scuffle to my right, I looked into the fireplace to see an eyeball staring at me. (We have a two-way fireplace from the kitchen to the family room.) My first thought was, "Egad! Daniel actually put his niece in the fireplace!" Then she came around the corner and I thought, "Oh no! She put the dog in the fireplace!" Then the dog appeared and I had run out of family members. Behind the glass doors, that frantic eye was still peering at me. Afraid to get too close, I squatted and from the light in the kitchen I could make out the form. It was a huge duck!

We had lived here less than two months and had already experienced far more than our share of bizarre nature experiences. We had discovered a super highway of moles in the backyard. A white-tailed deer had loped through the backyard during family time and we had our share of Canada goose doodles decorating the back yard. But this was too close. I had been making pizza for friends who were moving in that day and my dough and fixings covered the counters. I ran to the phone to call my husband at work to see if he had any suggestions.

"Oh, so that's what that sound was yesterday. I kept hearing things but I didn't see anything, so I thought it was the water cooler." Crazed duck, water cooler, sure, I guess they both sound the same when you're watching a basketball marathon and can't be bothered. As I was talking and making wisecracks about being the victim of fowl play, the duck decided that it had had enough and didn't like the way it looked behind glass, let alone under glass if the fireplace ignited. As it burst open the glass doors into the kitchen, my scream was bloodcurdling and scared me, my granddaughter, the dog, but mostly, the duck. I dropped the phone as the feathered wonder flew into the far window, fell, and then hopped through all the pizza fixings, leaving web prints everywhere. Grabbing my granddaughter and the dog, I first shoved the dog into her kennel and then flew up the stairs with my granddaughter under my arm. I reassured her as much as I could, turned on the TV in my room and told her to stay put. I would talk to her over the intercom and let her know what was happening.

My mind was racing but I knew I could not let it fly into the two-story foyer. I needed tools or weapons or something. From the linen closet, I extracted a mattress cover with gathered edges, thinking I could throw it over the duck and it would get caught in the elastic. Draping it like a mink stole over my shoulders, I picked up a broom and a mop on the way down the stairs, in case I had to bat it down first. By this time it could have been anywhere, but as I stepped into the kitchen doorway, I startled it and it took off into the eating area, knocking over everything in its path. Dropping to my knees, my plan unfolded. My purse was about ten feet away and my keys to the kitchen door were inside. I did my own pathetic version of the survival crawl to the purse, pulled the keys out, and dragged myself out of the kitchen toward the garage doors. Hearing the garbage truck coming down the street and being a woman of great creativity and little courage, I ran down the driveway still sporting my mattress pad and the weapons, one in each hand. Frantically, I explained what had happened and asked the two men if they might be able to offer some help. Evidently, they could not get past my combat uniform and they were laughing too hard to be of any assistance. Back to my plan.

I went around to the back of the house, skulked up the steps to the kitchen door and saw the intruder under the kitchen table, confused. It was so full of soot that I couldn't tell if it was male or female. I used the key to open the kitchen door and retreated to the bushes quickly. The blast of fresh air from the open door had no effect. Squatting behind the Mugo pines, I began to quack, hoping to lure the creature out the door. In case it was male, I used my most provocative quack, hoping he was up for some action and my call would send him flapping out the door. When that didn't work, I tried the compassionate quack, in hopes a female duck would be curious and come out to bond with a friend. In desperation, I tried the "I am a happy duck and I would like you to come out and play" quack, all the while hoping no neighbors were looking out their windows. Arms flapping, I tried my last quack, "I am so mad at you, you had better come out this instant or you are in big trouble, Mister." By this time my granddaughter had come out onto the second-floor balcony to watch her grandmother's antics. I assured her all would be well and it was almost over and please stay inside in case the duck ran amok.

The slam of a car door brought me to my feet and I headed for the driveway. Thinking and hoping that my husband had come home to save us and repent for his sins, I ran past the garage in my resplendent battle cape, still holding my weapons. It was not my husband, but our dear friend Greg on his way to meet the movers at their new home. My dearly beloved (and soon to be ex if he didn't have a VERY good reason for not coming to my aid) asked him to stop by on his way home because I had a "situation." Getting out of his car and coming up the driveway, he laughed and said that this was one of the best days of his life. Seeing little humor in the fact that my home had been taken over by a misguided bird, I apprised him of the situation and when he stopped laughing we went to the last place the duck had been seen. Like FBI agents checking a room for culprits, we slinked down the hall, looking left and right, covering each other's backs until we found the beast in the study. The bookshelves hadn't been delivered yet so there were boxes covering at least half the floor. He asked me to step out and close the glass door behind me.

What happened next was unbelievable. If I had closed my eyes, I would have sworn I was watching a Batman movie. BIFF! POW! CRASH! It all happened so fast, there was no time to think. Here was this wonderful human being, my hero, chasing and wrestling this wild, dazed fowl to the ground. Holding the duck down with an impressive half nelson (better than no nelson at all), he called for my mattress pad, finally, and we wrapped up the poor creature, took our bundle into the backyard, unfurled the pad and waited. Our feathered friend shook its entire body, looked over at us for a split second and took off through the trees to find his friends in the pond. It was over at last. The dog acted as though nothing had happened. My granddaughter appeared calm and unscathed. Of course, there were the duck prints in my pizza dough, and vegetables and sauce everywhere. I would have to start over.

A bond was formed that day with the Duck Man. He risked the wounds a wild duck might inflict with its bill, webbed feet or beating wings, with no thought for his personal safety. That's what I tell my husband when he tries to trivialize the whole event. No, the Duck Man and I will remember that day. Nothing can diminish it and I suspect, like me, he is experiencing post-traumatic duck syndrome. We don't talk about it but I can see it in his eyes and he can read me like a book. March 13th. It happened. We survived. It was a life-altering experience. Not a day goes by without something triggering an emotion from that event. In remembrance, on each anniversary, I break out my private bottle of Cold Duck. As I lift it to my lips in thanksgiving, I look into the fireplace to recall the events of that day. Here's to you, brave Duck Man. Long live the Duck Man.

Sentimental Journey — Well, The
Mental Part Is Right Anyway

Foot Soldier

While watching an especially animated episode of *working mom vs. stay at home mom* on Oprah one day, it struck me that women have not come very far at all in the world of feeling good about what they do. I'll be the first to tell you that my job as a mother is a terminal, full-time job. Cut and dried. The minute that first little bundle of joy slipped into this world, I was changed forever, for good or for bad. I've only run into a few women who were not fazed by the birth of their babies. It's normally a giant slap of reality and some women fall into it instinctively; some learn to dive in while others fight it, making sure everyone knows that this baby has not changed their essence, that motherhood is only a temporary phase.

These moms, on national television, were bent on convincing the other side and the viewing audience that their position was right, that it was an either/or situation. There were Geraldo Rivera moments during the show, when I thought someone would start throwing chairs and a melee of mothers would have to be separated from each other, still kicking and scratching to prove a point. Why do we have to convince anyone that we are right in the way we think or behave? As long as no one is harmed in the making of life's film, does it matter if we have approval from the rest of the world?

At fifty-six, I have to laugh at the antics I see new mothers go through because the more the world changes, the crazier the philosophies get. *Keep up with times,* the magazines tout, but the times change continually. It's a treadmill I got off of years ago. I wanted to live without rashes, guilt, or ulcers from making decisions that might or might not be vogue. My husband and I made a personal pact when we got married. He would go out, work and be the main breadwinner, and I would be in charge of the kids and transportation. We would move as needed to ensure he could advance in his career and our goal was, simply, to have enough money to educate the children. I would use my domestic talents to give back to the community what I could and to offer my quilting, sewing, craft, and floral wares at craft bazaars a few times a year. I was busy all the time and I felt very content because I was using my talents while not compromising my children. The point is that my husband and I made a personal pact. It worked for our family. I wouldn't expect it to be the answer for everyone. I would expect, however, that people would respect my choice as I would theirs. It has to be right for only you and your family. Before you think I was in control of everything from the start, I'd like to give you an example of a day in the life of this mother: good, bad, and ugly.

Without a second car, it was necessary to be very creative to get our errands done. I had one umbrella-type stroller at first, added a second, and finally ended up with three. Steering two at once was a little troublesome, but that third one caused some major problems with my steering ability. Long before the days of the plastic connectors, I carved (or whittled, if you will) wooden clips that would allow me to hook three strollers together, so we could get to preschool, swim classes, appointments, and everywhere else. We took up the whole sidewalk but I would politely turn sideways until the crowd cleared and onward we would push. When children numbers four and five arrived, I added a buggy to the fleet so I pushed the strollers with my left hand and pulled the buggy behind me with my right. We were lucky enough to adopt a baby shortly thereafter, and I wore her on my neck. The poor little thing had to hang on for dear life as both my hands were occupied with the vehicles and there were times I thought she would pull my hair straight out from clinging so hard. As we dropped kids off at various programs there was space for a few bags of groceries. We were limited to groceries approximately the weight of that child for each bag. The wheels on those fragile strollers wobbled at the slightest hint of imbalance and our goal was to arrive home without crippling any pedestrians. We took off, rain, shine, or snow each morning and got home in time for supper. People marveled at us; the mailman actually said he coveted my legs (I was hoping he meant the strength, not the shape), but few ever asked to be of assistance. There was no sense in complaining or whining. It was part of my pact. People honked at us all the time and the kids would wave like we were part of a parade. For times when speed was of the essence,

I had decked out my men's five-speed bike with child seats on front and back, a rickshaw thing that carried up to eighty pounds behind the bike and I fashioned a towel and foam "seat" on the bar so I could carry a maximum of five kids. I felt like a pack mule most times but we made our appointments on time. It was adventure every day.

Our move to California would turn out to be a blessing. Fresno is a very flat city in the San Joaquin Valley, sandwiched between L.A. and San Francisco. Summers average 110 degrees and it rains constantly in December and January. Most of the kids could ride by themselves by the time we got there and the city of Fresno actually has painted bike lanes in the right shoulders of the highways. I went everywhere on my bike, up to ten miles away for errands, but because of the flat surface, it was a piece of cake. We were there about a year when my husband's boss called him in to his office. He was concerned because I had been spotted all over town on a bike and he wanted to know why, unlike every other person in the valley, I was riding around in the intense heat instead of staying cool in my house or a car. His insinuation was that it was an embarrassment (to him or us?) that I had to ride a bike. My husband explained, simply, that we had only one car and I was used to doing this. A week later, my husband was awarded a company car and at the age of thirty-six I got my first big-girl car, a station wagon. The sky was the limit after that. What would I do with all the free time?

The schools were in need of room mothers (what's new?) and volunteers for everything else under the sun, so I filled up my day with those efforts. When the kids got sick, I was right there. It worked great, for me. All along my volunteer journey, people would say, "How can you stand this? How can you come every day and be so happy? Why don't you just get a job?" Can you imagine the number of personal phone calls I would have to field in a day? I did take a few teacher-assistant part-time jobs when the opportunity arose, but for the most part I offered myself happily to improve where I could. My husband was still on the move in his career and I was still in charge of kids and transportation. The kids were growing and the transportation part was much improved with the addition of the second car.

I can say with much joy that I did as much as I could in each place we lived, leaving behind quilts and christening gowns, auctioned for charities, more pizzas than I can count for school events, hundreds of patchwork tree skirts, aprons, floral pieces and Christmas decorations sold at craft fairs, and hours and hours of my personal time in volunteering. Only my husband and I know if I have honored our pact and it's only the two of us who should care. I volunteer in his name also, because he works hard enough and successfully enough for me to have the privilege of giving back. It has worked for us so far for thirty-five years. I look at my kids, all seven of them, and wonder what pact they will make to survive. I don't expect them to be like us. Everyone sees things differently, especially decades after our initial pact, and I just pray they'll come up with a good solution.

I'd be in big trouble if I was judged by my monetary impact. I look at my situation and think of myself in two ways. I am invaluable or I am worthless. I have chosen to be invaluable. No dollar amount on my head, and no one passing judgment on my accomplishments but me. If you ever looked at my closest friends, you'd find a wide assortment of women, all successful in what they do, whatever it is. Some are great businesswomen and can't boil water, while some can cook their hearts out, whip things up out of nothing, and understand little about business. There are even a couple of friends who appear to have both worlds under control. I love them all because they have hearts and souls that inspire me. We laugh like ninnies and get serious only when necessary. Do I think anyone should choose the pact I made with my husband? No, but before you decide, I'd be happy to let you see my legs. They've got at least fifty thousand miles on them and trust me, there's loads of "tread" left.

Fat Chance

FAT . . . It's everywhere . . . Two-thirds of Americans are overweight. It's the easiest thing to judge a person by — you don't need any additional information about them. It's right out there for you to see and immediately you know that this person has a defect. At least one aspect of their life is out of control. I have finally decided that it's time to do something about my condition. Why now? Despite all the medical information available, it was easy to turn a deaf ear because of the conflicting messages. Eat fat, don't eat fat. Eat beef, don't eat beef. Drink wine, don't drink wine. Exercise, but it only works at night. Exercise, but it only works in the morning. If the experts can't agree on anything, how is the average Joe or Jeannette supposed to figure any of this out? I've already purchased a lifetime pass for the roller coaster of dieting. I did the math a few months ago and realized that I have been overweight more years now than I've been thin and it started to annoy me. When did this roller coaster ride begin?

Athletics were a way of life for me before marriage. I played softball, volleyball and even basketball, although I am considered in the short range at 5'4". Beginner's luck was always my sidekick and I could pick up darts and succeed, or grab a bowling bowl and fare well. The only sport I couldn't conquer or even understand was golf. I'd swing my heart out and reach down to pick up the ball that had only dribbled a few feet forward. Miniature golf is a different story. A steady hand and a straight eye are all you need to win. The windmill is only there to confuse the meek.

In my all-girls high school, we played only volleyball and basketball and then had to suffer through modern dance in our attractive green shifts with bloomers. Transferring high schools in junior year gave me my first taste of sports like field hockey, gymnastics, lacrosse, and swimming. Swimming almost killed me. As a child I learned to swim in the Fox River where we shared the water with muskrats, snapping turtles, catfish, water moccasins, and other slimy things. I did not learn well but I learned fast. Pop up just once with a muskrat looking at you and you swim until you taste the sand on the beach.

At this new school, we were required to dive off the high dive to graduate. What! It was bad enough that I went from enclosed marble showers at my former school to the cattle drive shower where nothing was sacred and modesty was impossible. So, we were issued suits which I was grateful for since we heard that the boys swam sans suits. I tried everything she asked. I floated face up, face down, did the sidestroke, backstroke, butterfly and even the frog kick. Then came the day we were told to climb the stairs to the high dive. I never took drama but my performance is still talked about in the hallways today. I begged, pleaded for mercy, and came near to tears, telling her that I got butterflies driving over a paper bag. It was my intention to pass this course, but I could not, without risking permanent impairment or death itself, dive off that platform. The best I could achieve, I explained, was the worst belly flop in history, splaying my stomach contents to the bottom of the deep end. I would honor her by stepping off the platform but could not, would not dive. It sounded like a moral dilemma more than a physical challenge but she caved in. I won! I got a "B" and graduated without a black mark on my permanent record. I'm not proud of my cowardice but my instinct for self-preservation was born that day.

In college I started a women's volleyball league and our team was named "The Truck Driver's Union Express" and we all took names like Opal, Crystal, and Bertha to give it some authenticity. Our softball team was "Attila and the Hunnies" and I got to be Attila. There was activity all the time and the thought of gaining weight never entered my mind . . . until I got married.

There was no one to play with when my husband left for work. I used to take the dog out and try to get her to run, but she stopped at every blade of grass to sniff and add her donation. We lived in the tiniest town in Indiana and there just weren't many choices. Plus, my husband was a high school teacher and I had to behave myself or become the fodder for the teachers' lounge or locker room gossip.

Just three weeks into our marriage, I realized that you didn't have to be qualified to get pregnant, just present.

For the next four and a half months, the commode and I became very well-acquainted. Smells, sights, changes in balance from sitting to standing, and even breathing sent me to the ladies' room. My diet consisted solely of industrial-sized cans of fruit cocktail. It was the most pleasant thing to donate to the porcelain fixture and saved my esophagus from permanent damage.

The day that I sat up and did not have to make a bee line to the bathroom is a day I shall cherish forever. It was actually Christmas morning and certainly the best gift I could have received. I had lost over twenty-five pounds during these first months and thought I deserved some special treatment. Everything tasted so spicy compared to fruit cocktail that soon I was putting on pounds by the hour. I couldn't help it. My stomach growled non-stop and I was afraid to starve the baby. Imagine my surprise when I didn't give birth to a fifty-pound bundle of joy. I only lost two pounds after delivering a seven-and-a-half pound baby girl and at least as much in the aftermess. It wasn't fair! But baby and I walked and walked and I was within ten pounds of the old me when the news of baby number two arrived. With each baby I was an additional ten pounds further from the "old me" and after seven kids, there were a lot of cellulite mementos to hoist around. I tried exercise programs but there was always something that made me quit. Trust me, it didn't take much. My first low-carb diet was monitored by a doctor who held meetings for our group every Wednesday evening. I lost thirty pounds but with so few carbs, I also lost about thirty points off my I.Q. He used to talk while doing the box step at the same time, disturbing me. Step forward, right foot over left, step back, left foot over right, to the side, over and over and over. I wanted to hit him in the face with a pie. Of course, we would have all licked it off, being carb denied, but it was the repetition of the word "homeostasis" that drove me away from the diet and back to carbs. My friend Mary, who was my diet partner, swore she had the answer—the cabbage soup diet. After a week, she had enough gas to power a small city and smelled like someone died on her head. Thanks but no thanks.

Our parks and recreations department offered summer courses and I signed up for tennis, thinking it would help me in my quest to find the buried "me." We had four kids by then and my husband agreed to watch them for the hour. Kissing all of them goodbye and giving the baby an extra squeeze, I sauntered down the street to the tennis court. I was wearing shorts with a pre-stitched seam down the front and as I walked I felt for the seam. It was gone! Oh, wait . . . it's here in the back. I put my shorts on backward. I'm sure no one will notice. The instructor introduced himself and put us on doubles teams. I took the net and my partner said, "What's that on your back?" I pulled my shirt around to see that when I gave the baby the extra squeeze, he threw up down my back. So much for tennis.

Two kids later and we were moving to California. We got a house with a pool and I was much more excited about it than the kids. Every morning for three years I helped our son Joe with his paper route at 4:00 a.m. and by 5:00 I was in the water doing laps. I was up to eighty-five each morning before the kids heard water displacement and would come out to cannonball me. Still, I was working at it. I took an aerobics class at the high school and after two weeks, the school needed the room and we were going to have to disband. "Nonsense," I heard myself say. "We can do it at my house: Monday and Wednesday in the family room, and Friday in the pool for aqua-aerobics." It was perfect and we enjoyed many weeks of sweating and jogging in the pool. When the class was over, I joined a program where you ate real food and took supplements to help your metabolism. I was pretty sure my metabolism had long since jumped ship and was living in Cancun drinking piña coladas. My counselor's name was Misty and she was about eighteen and had just lost fifteen pounds, which qualified her as a counselor. She was the first Valley Girl I encountered and after a week I was eating Twinkies through the wrapper at the thought of having to listen to her voice. I requested a more experienced counselor, who happened to be a real estate agent in her other job. She was great until I mentioned we were moving and then her interest turned from my body to her possible agent percentage. Bye bye diet program.

I tried videos, but they were tortuous. Here's Jane Fonda twisting into positions I could only dream of and all the while, her deranged entourage is shrieking in excitement. Every move caused one of these noises and I had to stop exercising to see if someone had stepped on broken glass. Also, it was the beginning of that hideous diaper look and I had seen my share of diapers, trust me.

Richard Simmons could only be taken in very small doses and even Kathy Smith seemed to have bad posture and her group had one lady who looked down her own top excessively and one of the guys was in need of orthodontics. Was it the mother in me or the imperfection in them that left me cold on videos? Whatever, I felt pretty good about my progress and would continue my self-improvement pilgrimage and also see a doctor for lady issues when our move was complete.

My trip to the doctor in Illinois was quite productive. It appeared I could have been the estrogen poster girl for the last ten years as progesterone had joined my metabolism in Cancun and was considered AWOL. Three sessions of little teeny pills and I was a regular woman in the woman department. I was so busy celebrating normal cycles that I barely noticed my husband's excitement at the new, thinner, less-PMS-riddled me. One normal cycle was all I would enjoy. Pregnant for the seventh time at forty, I said goodbye to my body and embarked on my nine-month path of expansion. We moved (again) right in the beginning of the third trimester and for exercise I mowed our new one-acre lawn, unpacked, and rearranged our possessions and told myself I'd get back to me sooner or later.

Later it is, and the baby is fifteen. We've all been watching our diet, trying the low salt, no sugar, no wheat diet and the weight is dropping off. I had a personal trainer come to my home to teach me how to use my household appliances to get in shape.

If nothing else made me see how necessary good health is, a visit from my grandchildren was all I needed.

I swam with the baby at the pool, and attended a music class with her where we stood up and sat down a zillion times, nestled under a parachute tent and danced the Toddler Tango. It's worth it to be in shape for my own health, for my kids' sake, but those little ones are the killers. One of the little girls in our swim class, whose mother was pregnant, asked, innocently, "Why are YOU fat?" She probably guessed I was too old to be pregnant. Her mother was mortified but I replied, "That's a very good question. I've spent the last thirty-five years taking care of everybody else and it's finally my turn to take care of me." She probably wasn't interested in my long-winded response but I was so happy to report that a change was in the wind.

My new best video friend is Leslie Sansone. She has young and older participants alike walking with her and even a token male. No one has an overbite and hardly anyone is fixated on their bosom. Really. I've been looking for a reason to stop and so far, no luck. She's a normal mom with three kids and her body is human. If I had to criticize one thing, it would be the outfits they wear. Everyone is color coordinated for the most part, but in the three-mile walk, Randy is wearing something that does not blend well with the others. I try not to look in that direction. Sometimes I do the one and the two mile together so I don't have to see it. I've even tried turning backwards and just listening but it's impolite to turn your back on friends. I'll try pasting a little black pair of paper shorts over him on the TV screen to see if it makes a difference. I can't switch anymore. I don't own anything steel-worthy—not buns, thighs, or abs—and those commercials make me think he should cut down on the caffeine. Richard is still wearing the same pink striped shorts and couldn't his family spring for a few electrolysis treatments? I've got to stay focused and remain strong. Hostess has just come out with the Willy Wonka purple and orange cupcakes and they looked awfully enticing on my granddaughter's face. My granddaughter . . . now I remember why I am committed to this. I'll think of all four grandchildren when Randy's shorts get on my nerves. I'll be fine. But, just in case, hide the cupcakes.

Lost and Found

A t least half of my day is spent looking for things,
items I had in my hands just minutes before they
disappeared. Eyeglasses, bills, credit cards,
clothing and especially car keys were either misplaced by
me or, I suspect, grabbed by my band of merry children to
be part of some stolen treasure for their games. It was bad
enough B.C. (before children) but things picked up when
my "mommy" activity level escalated. I'd be heading
towards the goal line with item in hand and either the
phone would ring, a fracas would break out, the
washer/dryer buzzer would sound or one of the animals
would commit an atrocity that needed my immediate
attention. I'd lay the item down, sure I would remember
the logical place where I was putting it, and then spend
the rest of the day trying to figure out what my reasoning
was when I put it down. I've already confessed that I was
not into fastidious house organization. The "House of
Piles" would pretty much describe our style.

The kids thought it was a fun game. What did mommy
lose now? Is there a reward? We'd search the house top to
bottom, turning things over, making an even bigger mess

and I'd finally give up. Just short of age thirty, six little ones aged seven and younger, and I was flirting with a breakdown brought on by the frustration of losing everything I touched. Hanging on with white knuckles to the edge of sanity, I'd pray to God that the madness would cease before I did. As a Roman Catholic girl taught by nuns through grade school, I was instructed to call on the saints and the Holy Family in good times and in bad. I felt guilty about taking up God's time with my trivial problems when he had world peace conflicts on His plate. His mother, Mary, had never let me down, but again, she had some pretty big issues like communism to deal with. I'd have to find some saints less busy, even use my own family members who had passed and perhaps had not yet received full-time heavenly employment.

One of the requirements of attending Catholic school, right after mastering the "These Are Your Friends" series with David, Ann and Spot, was to familiarize yourself with the *Lives of the Saints* book. It is a comprehensive life account of every saint and we were asked, throughout elementary school, to give presentations on particular ones, especially the saint after whom we were named. There were at least four volumes in the set and there was a saint for every purpose, every need. Given my present dilemma, I was sure I would need a swat team of saints so I paged through and came up with my Heavenly Dream Team, the group that would bring me in off the ledge and save what was left of my sanity. Almost everyone knows that Saint Anthony is the "finder" saint. If you lose something, a call to him usually leads you right to the item.

Again, enter guilt. So sure he would get sick of my whining along with everyone else's, I thought I should enlist a few others. He was a pretty busy saint. Also, I felt bad that he had such a lame poem assigned to him. "Tony, Tony, turn around. There is something to be found"— hardly a Shakespearean moment. But he'd make a good captain. Saint Jude, Danny Thomas's saint of choice, is the patron saint of hopeless or difficult cases. I thought my problems qualified for hopeless and I enlisted him and added a lesser known saint, Joseph of Cupertino, also renowned for his help with the hopeless. I signed them up as a tag team. My last choice was St. Lucy, patron of the blind. Every time we'd look for something and complain to our mother that it really wasn't anywhere, she'd say "Saint Lucy help you. It's right under your nose. You just can't see it because you're not looking hard enough." So, my holy quartet chosen, it was time to put them to the test. Now there's something you should know about saints. They've already been tested and have passed with flying colors, so they don't need to mess with everyday earthly problems if they don't feel like it. It's best to be humble when asking for help so you don't aggravate them. They also have great senses of humor and like to play with you, test your faith and just drag you around for the sport of it. You've got to love these guys.

My first test was the day I had to take the kids with me for a doctor's appointment. I had my keys out on the table and I was getting socks and shoes on the last child when I heard the keys jingling. "Don't play with Mommy's keys. We have to leave right away. We can't be late for the doctor." Silence. The jingling stopped. A bad sign. I raced to the last known spot and sure enough, no keys. I had colored keys made especially so I could find them easier but they had just disappeared. The toddler in question, the jingler, smiled sweetly and gave me the "I don't know" shrug. Nooooooo. Not today. The kids all had the "not me" look. Okay, the time had come to test my new saintly crew in the finding of the keys. I sat at the kitchen table and put my hands in my face. "I give up. Really. I can't do this by myself. I need you. Please." I sat up and breathed, letting all the air out of my lungs. As if pulled up by my nostrils, I began walking and went out of the kitchen, through the dining room, into the living room and towards the front door. Were they going to throw me out of my own house? I walked over to the umbrella stand, a place I had looked a hundred times in the last few minutes. There was one umbrella, a clear one with giant red and blue circles on it and I lifted it up. I had taken all of them out before but this time I opened that one and way down deep in the metal mechanism was my set of red, blue, and silver keys. I couldn't believe it! It worked. Thank you, thank you, thank you, team. I danced and the kids joined in. They had no idea why I was so happy, but that was the day my sanity got a second chance. It's been twenty six years and they've never let me down. That doesn't mean they don't toy with me or play tricks on me. They probably get pretty tired helping me find my lost articles. They even tell me if there's no hope looking. "Don't you remember you threw it out, saying you hadn't used it in ten years?" I take their tricks and laugh right along with them because it's a small price to pay for the work they do for me. They hardly ever take it too far.

I was heading to a scrap-booking open house and had my car jammed with books, stickers, pens and tape. The community center was reserved by a friend who had given me the keys to get in early. The entry gate was locked and the keys I had only opened the main door so I used my cell phone and reported the problem. I put the phone in a safe place and continued to unpack the car. About fifteen minutes later, I needed to make a call and could not locate the phone. Anywhere. I found a payphone and called my own phone. Nothing. Then I dialed my daughter. I instructed her to call the cell twice, at three minute intervals, so I could check the car and then the room. Nothing again. As the night went on, I asked my friends to be on the look out but it was nowhere to be seen. Four hours later, as we packed up, we checked every box, every bag and even went through the garbage. The path I traveled was limited to a hallway and the small room and there was no way I could have lost it. Frustrated and totally humble by this time, I raised my eyes and hands heavenward and said, "Okay, I give up. I hope you have had your fun but I'm too pooped to care now. Help me, please. At least give me a hint." With that, my right hand came down and crossed over to my left breast like I was about to start the Pledge of Allegiance. "Okay. Thanks." I reached into my bra, Italian grandma style and pulled out a very hot, moist cell phone. It had been cooked by my body heat, but my friends were more in shock about me not feeling it and them not seeing it at all during the evening. It was the days before the mini-phones and it was at least six inches long plus a three-inch pencil-width antenna. I could hear the saints laughing up a storm as I tried to explain that the kids had pummeled and poked me so much throughout my mommy years that pain and discomfort were a part of my daily routine. I'd have to be pushed down the stairs to feel any sensation anymore. I was a little surprised, though, that I didn't even feel the vibration when the phone rang as my daughter and I placed several calls. There was nothing left to say. I was about as humbled as I'd ever been and I made them pinky swear that they'd keep this our little secret. It took six days for the phone to work again, with a little help from my hair dryer. Now, I'm not selfish and I am happy to share this group with anyone who could use their help. Even my friends who are unbelievers are stunned by the outcome of their requests. Just make sure you are prepared for the practical jokes. They have to get something for all their trouble, even if it's just a few good stories to tell St. Peter as he awaits his next customer at the Pearly Gates.

Accidentally Speaking

I've been driving for over forty years and my record is pretty good. I got my first speeding ticket the day my first child got her driver's license. The bathroom at the licensing station was out of order and my anxiety for her success had taken its toll on my bladder. The officer was not concerned that I was about to leak all over my car and that was that. I went home to the moving truck in my driveway and kissed California goodbye the next day, sending payment for the ticket by mail. Twenty-two years of driving before my first ticket.

Four years later, I would receive the most absurd ticket ever. While I was on vacation, some misguided politician was talked into placing a "No Thru Traffic" sign inside a subdivision that was the only safe way to get from our house to the high school. I had dropped my son off at football practice and headed home the usual way. I noticed the flashing lights and pulled over. "Didn't you see the sign?" he asked. "What sign?" I asked dumbfounded. "You can't drive through here anymore." He handed me a ticket and grumbled about wasting his time on this dumb assignment when there were crooks to catch and donuts to eat. I went back to the entrance to look for a sign. Several homes were under construction, one right at the entrance of the subdivision. There were derricks, bulldozers, torn up sidewalks; it was a mess. Amidst the mess was the new sign. How was I supposed to see it? I raced home to get my camera and started snapping shots of the street outside the subdivision, at the entrance and exit.

On the appointed date, I went to the courthouse for my hearing, folder in hand. There were at least one hundred fifty other people there for the same reason, and the bailiff said there were at least that many the night before and as many were expected the next night. What a goldmine for the city, I thought. Nearly five hundred people paying for stupid tickets. They could build a new courthouse with the proceeds. Rabble rouser that I am, I tried to mount an offense, telling them that I had proof the tickets were invalid. I had a loophole! The prosecuting attorney came out just about then and announced that they were willing to change the charge to "loud and excessive muffler noise" or something equally as absurd. It would be reduced to a non-moving violation. We'd plead guilty to the lesser charge and get no points on our driving record. Each of us had to pass by the judge and say "guilty" or "not guilty." I had already counseled some out-of-state people that they should not get a ticket for looking for a new home in that subdivision. They got off and went home but everyone else fell for the diminished charge and they were all willing to pay the fine plus court costs. Except yours truly. I was stunned and the judge looked at me like I was nuts when I said, "Not guilty, Your Honor. My muffler works fine. Is that even legal?" The whole place cleared out and I was left alone to face Night Court.

Night Court consisted of the judge, the assistant DA, the ticketing police officer, and me. The assistant DA was miffed that I didn't take the plea bargain and set out to humiliate me. The police officer was first to take the stand. "Do you see the perpetrator of the crime here tonight, officer?" "Yes, there she is there," he said pointing to me, the only person in the courtroom. I looked around to make sure I was alone and had to chuckle. He didn't know me from Adam. "Did you give her a ticket on this day in August?" "Yes I did," he replied firmly, a great deal of pride in his voice. "No more questions, Your Honor."

The judge looked at me and asked if I had any questions for the officer. "Just one, if it pleases the court." Turning to the officer, I asked, "How many tickets have been issued since this sign went up?" "I object, Your Honor. Leading the witness." "Okay, then, can you tell me if the roads through this subdivision are paid for with my tax money? Is it not a public thoroughfare?" "Objection, your honor. Irrelevant." She really did not play well with others. Finally I said, "No more questions, Your Honor," and took the stand myself. It was personal now. There was no way I could let her win. She started all this garbage about me thinking I was above the law. I produced my pictures of the area, taken the day of the incident, and the judge was eager to see them. "Your Honor," she begged, "this is just a ploy on her part to get out of paying her ticket." "I object, Your Honor. Argumentative." By this time the judge was having a good time with me.

I had laid out the pictures to tell the story. There were no signs outside the subdivision at either end indicating that thru entry was prohibited. By the time you turned in, and assuming you were in a moving vehicle, your attention turned to the construction constraints. The sign was eleven feet four inches tall and you would have had to be in a convertible or possessed the neck of a giraffe to see it. The signs outside the subdivision were placed there more than six weeks after the first tickets were issued. I recounted how the residents were selling lemonade and cookies while they clapped at each ticket-giving opportunity. I even insinuated that someone might have been paid off or coerced to put the signs up. Perhaps the councilman lived in the subdivision himself and was hoping for reelection. "I object, Your Honor." The DA was getting on my nerves now. Finally the judge asked, "Do you have anything further to add to this case?" "That she won't object to? Probably not, but let me say this, Your Honor. I am a mother to seven children, four of whom have their licenses. My first rule for them and myself is to be totally responsible while driving. I would not knowingly commit a crime nor would I allow my children to get away with one. I am a law-abiding citizen and this is a travesty to the American judicial system. I am sorry the court has to waste its time on such nonsensical matters." Perry Mason, move over. I was on a roll. The judge lost little time in his response. "I am very glad you brought the pictures with you as evidence. I now have a better understanding of the predicament and the area in question. I have no choice but to dismiss the charges. You will not pay for the ticket and you will not be responsible for any court charges. You are free to go." I thanked him, curtsied, and walked outside. The police officer was the first person I saw. "Thank God someone finally said something. You did a great job," he added. I was feeling a little giddy when the crabby assistant DA approached me. "You are so lucky you got away with it. He must have been in a good mood. You could have gotten two points against your driving record and your insurance would have gone up." It was sour grapes, pure and simple. I would have still had ten points to play with, sister. I waited until I got in the car to do the victory whoop.

Half the staff at the high school had received tickets as well and all of them paid around two hundred dollars for lawyers and fines. They were stunned that I got off without paying a cent. I asked them how they could live now with their driving records blemished. I'm not sure I should associate with people who have been convicted of loud and excessive muffler noise. What a laugh . . .

Now that was fourteen years ago and until December I was accident free. I was at a stoplight behind about a dozen cars when WHAM! I was hit from behind by a young man who jumped out, startled. "What happened?" I asked him in shock. "You stopped," he said accusingly. "We call that a red light in almost every state, I believe. The dozen people ahead of me would probably agree." He was sixteen, driving too fast and like most teenagers, had most of his hormones in his gas-pedal foot. Still, it wasn't my fault and I was not issued any type of ticket. I'm afraid my accident-free days are coming to an end, though. I just got a new car with a sun roof and I can't help but notice something. I have a lot of gray hair. Look, there's one there . . . and there. Oh, there's another one. Look at that one. It's wiry and sticking straight up. Is that one gray, too? No, it's just the sunlight . . . or is it? Stop honking. I can see the light is green, but I just found another gray hair . . .

Nightmare

With all the modern inventions and conveniences available, you'd think there'd be something for the phenomenon I experienced going out to dinner this past weekend. True, I didn't lose the fifty pounds I had hoped in the ten days prior to the occasion, but I did find a new dress and bought the "buy four, get two free" pantyhose deal while I was at it, just to cover all my bases, and hopefully, my carcass. On the back of the panty hose box is a grid that explains how to pick the perfect size for your body. There are hundreds of little boxes to choose from and there is always the hold-your-breath moment when you drag your finger down the height column, bear to the right as it meets the weight row, and (according to the color of your box) find the letter of the alphabet that corresponds to your body shape. Your hope is to be in the A to C range, but unless you are a stick figure you know it will be the D, E, or F letter that fits your proportions. Of course, the colors in my size were limited to Pasty Pale Anemia, Varicose Vein Purple, Burnt Coffee Grounds Brown, Cruella de Ville Basic Black and Freddie Krueger Friday the Thirteenth Red. My dress is full length so I have some leeway here. I choose two of the Burnt Coffee Grounds color (the closest to human leg color if you live by the equator) and one of each of the others, then head home to prepare for the evening.

It's a special dinner with people I've not met before and I always try to look like I'm capable of handling an adult moment. It's not as easy as it sounds. I prepare for these occasions as if I am attending the prom, and although my dress will cover my legs, I attempt the shaving process in case there's intense wind. It's been decades since my legs looked like legs. The shaving process is crude, but if I bend over to get a good look at the situation, I'll black out from cutting off my circulation to the waist and it could get uglier. I solve the problem by tying my shaver to a dragline, casting it down towards my ankles and pulling it back up to my knees. The outcome is always a surprise and more often than not resembles those mysterious patterns found in cornfields, but I call it art and go on with the process.

I gave up makeup and jewelry in the '70s when my loving children massacred my smear-proof blusher and tore my earrings and pearl necklace from my body in one deft, ninja move. So after washing my face, I check (with my reading magnifiers on) for any rogue facial hairs which are a birthright and plague of women over fifty who have Mediterranean genes. Finding none, and running short on time, I begin the process of dressing. Feeling frisky, I choose the Cruella de Ville black pantyhose and notice the handy dandy cotton crotch that excuses you from wearing underpants. Yeah, like I'm going to fall for that one. A good wind and all your mysteries are revealed in a pressed-ham-under-glass sort of way. I don my industrial undies and size up the panty hose, which don't look like they could cover a bud vase. I test the stretchability, knowing that I will tax them beyond their limits even though I am well within the comfort zone on the size chart. They have tummy control, which means there are steel bands across the front that push your stomach in, forcing the flesh to find a home elsewhere. If you turn around and take a look at your back side, you know exactly where the excess is now living. The new proportions of my butt notwithstanding, I consider the proper stance to begin the torturous ordeal of one foot at a time, shimmy, shimmy, pull, massage as you go up. It's a good thing I remembered to take a Dramamine earlier, as the swaying and rotating will surely make me nauseous. The pantyhose are only to my knees when the cotton crotch begins to show the strain, leading me to believe that there is much more leg than there is fabric. Heading back down to the ankles to massage any excess upwards toward the promised land, the inevitable thought crosses my mind — there is no reasonable way to test these panty hose on real people (who would succumb to the degradation?), so the fact that they're not going to make it easy on me no longer surprises me. I'm within inches of the waistband of my industrial undies. The color, no longer black, has faded to spotty gray from the stress, but I gyrate in an undulating fashion to coax them to their final resting place. I make a mental note to have absolutely nothing to drink during the evening because I don't have the strength to pull them up twice in a twenty-four-hour period. I grab my thirty-year-old panty girdle (insurance that everything will stay put for the evening) and can't get it up fast enough. A slinky half slip assures that my dress will glissade over any leftover bumps and I am ready. Until I take my first step. Somewhere on the journey, the pantyhose twisted just enough to abrade my flesh in the same area that friction would ordinarily start a fire if I had to run for any distance. There's no time to start over, so I practice taking baby steps to keep the pain at bay. My eyes are bulging from the pressure of the control top but out we go.

At the restaurant, everything begins well. We are introduced, share pleasantries, I refuse the glass of wine (due to the no liquid stipulation) and after a half-hour wait, we are seated, ready for a wonderful evening of food and conversation. No sooner has the waiter laid the napkin across my lap than the ugly mutiny begins. My slip slithers over my stomach in a southerly direction and settles somewhere unknown. Still, three layers of protection, no problem. A few minutes later, the tried and true trusty panty girdle that saw me through all my postpartum lumps and bumps begins to shudder from the pressure and it, too, heads for the border. Very uncomfortable from the fabric bunching up, I make the biggest mistake: I squirm to readjust—and that's when I earn the Academy Award performance of my life. I pretend to be interested in the story being told about a fabulous experience in Switzerland and all the while I'm pulling an Arnold Schwarzenegger, trying to hold my pantyhose up by repeatedly expanding and contracting my stomach muscles. Once compromised by this movement, the steel band gives way and dives below to be with the other garments, and only seconds later my undies, unwilling to stand alone, take the plunge also. It is both frightening and freeing. The pressure is gone but now the fear possesses me — by dessert my entire foundational system will be somewhere around my ankles. Thank God for the full-length dress. I can squat and walk out of the restaurant as no one but my husband knows how tall I am and he stopped asking questions and noticing things years ago. Hugs are exchanged, goodbyes are delivered, and I waddle to the waiting car, struggling to climb up into our SUV swiftly before my condition is revealed to the valet and unsuspecting diners. Once in the vehicle, I writhe and contort, much to my husband's shock, as I wriggle out of the confining objects of my torture. A stickler for being a law-abiding citizen, I squelch the idea of throwing all of it out the window on our way home. No, the traitors don't deserve getting off that easy. Instead, they will live to serve another day. I will string the pantyhose to a four-poster twin bed. It will just have to learn that it absolutely must meet the standards advertised on the envelope. We can't endorse this kind of mediocrity.

I will boil my panty girdle in hopes it will regroup and sign on for another thirty years. There isn't much hope for my granny underwear and the slip, so I will employ suspenders or duct tape to handle them. Then it hits me. I could have avoided all of this if I had bought the can of spray tan instead of all the panty hose. They might not make that product in black, but Rustoleum has a flat black that might work. I have some left from refinishing the bathtub I use for a planter in the backyard. In fact, I have paint in lots of colors from projects around the house. A gallon of turpentine and some cotton towels, and I think I've got something here. It just might work.

Ahoy, Maties

My husband was feeling guilty that he had already experienced his lifetime dream of a trip to Kenya and my dream of a whale-watching excursion had not come to pass. For my birthday, he presented me with a glossy picture of a hundred foot, three-masted sailing schooner that would be my home for a six-day cruise around Martha's Vineyard, Nantucket, and Provincetown, with a final stop at Cutty Hunk. There was a whale-watching moment included on the trip and he said I could choose a sailing partner as long as it wasn't him. He was heading on a week's stay with our two oldest sons, Joe and Mark, on a true cowboy outing in Utah and was sure he wouldn't have anything left for a sailing cruise. I said that the next person to call and wish me a happy birthday would be my traveling mate, and thirty seconds later my oldest sister Mary Ann was jumping for joy that she remembered to call.

We flew to Providence, Rhode Island and were driven to Newport, where we spent the night in an old prison, turned hotel. The next day we appeared on the dock with far too much luggage, waiting for the tender to take us to our floating hotel. We could see it way offshore, too large to moor any closer and as we got into the tender we were told that the ten of us would be the only ones on the forty-passenger ship. Eight crew members would round off the list and off we would sail. As landlubbers, my sister and I had taken an anti-motion-sickness pill and we were glad as several passengers were experiencing a bit of tummy turmoil. We boarded the ship and were shown to our quarters. Quarters, indeed. In this case it was eighths or sixteenths as the rooms couldn't have been smaller. They were more like closets with bunk beds and because of my claustrophobia, Mary Ann was kind enough to call the top bunk. On her back, the tip of her nose was less than an inch from the ceiling, something that would have caused me to jump ship. The closet was humorous, more like a large business envelope, but the bathroom took the prize. You could sit on the toilet or take a shower or both at the same time. It was quite the creative use of space, really, but we made the mental note to distinguish between the flush button and the shower head button.

Once unpacked, we were invited to the captain's opening remarks. We were introduced to the crew, most of them younger than my children. The captain and the chef were a married couple but they promised "no canoodling" and we took them at their word. Our ship, the *Arabella,* once belonged to Kelly McGillis (the actress) and after a fire, it was sold, sliced in half, forty feet of galley and cabin space added and was now quite the belle of the sea. We got our sailing lesson ("Don't fall off the ship") and we prepared to sail. There were three couples who were traveling together for the cruise, one mom/daughter team and the odd couple, Mary Ann and me. The crew was ready to please and offered Bloody Marys as we set sail. Having had the anti-motion-sickness pill, we declined and in an hour we were the only ones still conscious. It was like a personal tour with only ten passengers aboard, so we had the run of the ship and could move and find a seat wherever we went. Glorious is the only word that fits the feeling of gliding across the water with the wind. I sat in the back (the aft?) in front of the American flag waving proudly in the breeze. Right next to me was the hot tub which we were free to use when we anchored. My husband called to see how things were going and I answered the phone with "Hello, greetings from heaven. How may I help you?" and it got better from there.

Every morning we set sail and each night we moored offshore and could go into the town for dinner if we liked. Mary Ann, the shopper, was only too glad to hit the shopping scene whenever possible. By the second day we were sleeping with all our purchases piling up at the ends of our bunks. It didn't matter. I was preparing for my big moment.

In a few days I would get my opportunity to see whales. Whales, mind you. Extraordinary, gigantic, beautiful whales. Nothing else mattered. I would get my wish soon enough. On the brochure, it mentioned a "whale-watching experience" but it turned out to be a "maybe we will and maybe we won't" kind of thing. It seems that whales pretty much have control over what they do and where they go and they can travel quite the distance in the hunt for food. Captain Joel promised me he would do his best to honor my dream. To while away the time, we played Scrabble with Sonja and Katya, mother and daughter recently here from Russia. They had been playing with the other couples who were sticklers about spelling and the ladies, being new to the U.S., were spelling phonetically. We had given up playing with the couples when they tried to pass off some "Texas-isms" on us and when a look in the dictionary found no such word, they grumbled and let the crew fix them some more drinks. They had also invited us to a limerick contest and then held it in secret, acing us out. The grand prize was a toe ring from Provincetown, Massachusetts, and while I disapprove of metal cutting off the circulation to one's toes, it was the principle of the matter. I expressed my displeasure and they challenged me to recite, at that moment, the limerick I authored within seconds of the first invitation. Just so you know I really did it, here is my pitiful donation to the contest:

There once was a girl from Nantucket
Whose tummy she thought she should tuck it
Her husband said, "No"
Her doctor said, "Whoa"
So she said, "What the heck, I'll just suck it"

With that I sucked my tummy in as far as I could and it got a good laugh. It certainly wasn't stellar but it did earn me an honorary toe ring. One day closer to my whales.

I have to admit that I have not traveled very extensively and I find it necessary to learn everything I can on a trip. I was last to go to bed at night and first up every morning. At night I asked the crew about their lives and how they came to crew on the *Arabella*. I got all their stories and felt like I was with family in a few days. Mornings I would get up, slip my swimsuit cover up over my head so as not to disturb my sleeping sister and head to the railing to watch the trappers come and check the cages, retrieving lobsters for the most part. Each trapper had a different colored buoy, which most times were just painted, plastic gallon milk jugs. They never said a word or even looked up from their task.

We were supposed to file past the food bar for meals but because I got up first and alone, I was served breakfast personally each day. It was such a luxury and something I was very grateful for. My poor sister, thin as a rail, didn't bring enough warm clothing and could not stay up late without being chilled to the bone. She was also a late sleeper so I stayed up top until she came up for her breakfast. I would run down, shower and reappear in minutes, not wanting to miss a drop of water or piece of seaweed.

Here it was—my day of days. Captain Joel promised he would do his best to find out where whales were running and he would guide the *Arabella* in that direction. He told us there were two types of whales in the area—right whales and humpbacks. He headed for Stellwagen Bay, our best hope for the day. I had my camera ready, lots of rolls of film for my little 35mm camera, and I went to the very front (bow?) to be the lookout. An hour passed before I thought I saw something. It looked like the tip of a whale's fluke. A few minutes later, I thought I saw a whale spew from the blow hole (that sounds really awful, doesn't it?) and I yelled what I've been dying to yell for years. "Thar she blows," I uttered triumphantly, grabbing my camera. There seemed to be more than one and as we headed in that direction, the captain cut the engines completely and tuned into his radio for more information. Another ship reported a family of humpbacks nearby: mother, father and yearling. We were within fifty feet of them when a whale tourist boat came out of nowhere, making all kinds of noise, distracting the whales. I yelled to the captain, "Does our boat's bottom look more like a whale than their boat's bottom? Does my bottom look more like a whale, because I'll go in if it makes a difference?" He assured me that it would pay off if we were patient. Finally, the tourist boat left and the whale family came over to our ship. I was snapping pictures, left and right, making dolphin noises because I couldn't get a believable whale noise to come out. They were playing with us, going under the boat, rolling over to show their white underbellies and coming up on the other side. I must have been hanging over the boat with my feet hooked around the rails because I have a picture of the mother whale at the side of the boat as she popped up, looking at me, smiling. Honest. Our eyes met and she knew. We bonded at that moment. I was so happy I thought about jumping in. She submerged to be near the yearling and we all ran up to the bow to watch the father whale flap his fluke. (Say that three times fast.) Mary Ann's camera ran out of film and I offered one of my twenty-five rolls but she ran down to the cabin to get more. Just then Andi, the chef, announced lunch. "In a minute," we all chanted and stayed as near to the whale as we could get. Ready to join his family, the father whale gave us one last salute. He spewed an enormous amount from his blow hole and it was going to land on all of us. We were excited, getting ready for the saltwater spray. Picture, if you will, mostly clear liquid diarrhea cascading on the lot of us. Our spins of joy turned to screams of horror as we were all covered in the stench of a lifetime. The captain nonchalantly advised us that if we ate fish every day and never brushed or flossed our teeth, we would probably have breath much like that of whales. That was information worth knowing ahead of time. The only one not affected, of course, was Mary Ann who came up on deck, camera reloaded, and asked what stunk so badly. "All of us!" we screamed as we headed for the lunch line and rubbed the ice from the salad bar all over ourselves until the smell dissipated. Our clothes were so awful I took advantage of that toilet/shower option and rinsed the stink off while tending to other matters. But it didn't faze me. I could have enjoyed more hours, even more days with the whales. My moment had come and gone but I would have the pictures to show for it.

In a wild moment on the second to last day, they invited me to try my hand at steering the boat. The engines were running and they put me at the ship's wheel. I thought I had the hang of it when I noticed that land was propelling towards us in a rather swift fashion. "Uh, guys, I don't see any brakes. How do you stop this thing?" They laughed and took their sweet time coming to my aid, but we sailed gently into the bay at Cutty Hunk, population thirty-five, I believe. We were treated to a lobster and potato dinner over coals, my first ever, and two very sweet teens guided me through the process of getting my money's worth. Lobster was flying everywhere and a good time was had by all. We stayed overnight in the bay and awoke for our final sailing day with thunderstorms brewing. I received this information ten minutes after I was treated to the final breakfast—eggs benedict. They were predicting twelve-foot swells but not to worry. The ship had survived swells of over thirty feet with no problems. My sister and I each took two anti-motion pills and braced for the fun. It was everything you've seen in movies where a ship is being tossed around like a toy. Most of the passengers went inside to the dining area or into their cabins but I found it better to look into the horizon for stability than peer through a portal with water sloshing back and forth in so tiny a circle. Actually it was a perfect ending. Five days of paradise and back to the reality of the real world. Two and a half hours later we landed and were tendered soaking wet to shore. Two very nice passengers allowed us to change out of our wet clothes in their hotel room in town. We shopped and had lunch in a motion-pill stupor and our limo ride to Boston must have been some treat for the driver. We passed out, mouths open and drooling for the entire trip, although I think he shared the sights with us in case we could hear him. We were still shaky with sea legs as we took the bus tour around Boston and the sensation was much like that last day's tossing. I woke up clutching the side of my bed both mornings and all my dreams were filled with the ship's rocking sensation. It took until we got on the airplane for our return trip to feel balanced again. I thought about my experience with the whales, the highlight of the trip. Everything was perfect, right up until the spewing incident. I might just call the coast guard to see how cost effective it would be to drop breath mints by the tons into the waters around the areas where whales interact with humans. It just might help a whale's social life. I would imagine that bad breath is a turn off with almost every species. Trust me, I'll donate big time to the fund.

Resolutions

New Year's Day. Time for that age-old tradition—resolutions! If you're like most, you make a list that, if you followed successfully, would earn you a pair of wings, a halo, and a jet trip to the pearly gates. The trouble is that life has a funny way of interrupting your intentions. Here's a typical list of one poor, misguided soul's resolutions:

Lose weight. (Number one on almost everyone's list every year since time began.) You swear that this will be the year, nothing can stop you, do you hear me? NOTHING! And you actually mean it until about noon when the first bowl game begins and you find yourself hip deep in the dip. You didn't mean to slip, but the pre-game show is so riveting . . .

Get organized. As if it's possible, you begin by opening *the* kitchen drawer, you know the one. How hard could it be to conquer *one* little drawer? Memories overwhelm you as you fondle each item, much too valuable to throw out. A hair clip, a screw from something or other, matches from that wedding where the bride's gown could have doubled as the main mast for a ship, a flashlight with dead batteries. Three hours later, the drawer is empty but the counter is cluttered with these same objects. There is no home save the one they recently vacated. All but the lint ball are put safely back. You'll assess the situation again next year.

Scour the refrigerator. This year there will be NO leftovers to fester in the far recesses of the bottom shelf. The whole neighborhood counts on me to supply their children with primo science projects from inside there — well, those days are over! As I open the door, I hear something hissing and I can see something else migrating to another container. Maybe this isn't the day to tackle a project this large. I open an industrial-sized box of baking soda, set it on the top shelf, and before I can close the door, I swear I see it shudder. It looks like another great year for science.

Tame the closets. Face it, sister. No one is going to ask to wear your old maternity clothes. No one will sport your polyester bell-bottoms (except on Halloween) and the last time you wore size 8½ shoes, Jimmy Carter was apologizing for having lustful thoughts. But you *know,* as soon as you give them away, someone's going to ask for them. Their lives are spared but they do get pushed a little further back on the rack. It's vintage clothing by now, isn't it?

Start Exercising. There are twenty-four hours in a day, right? At least one of them should be spent outdoors, walking. Of course, that means new shoes, sweats, picking a time before 6:00 a.m. so the neighbors don't have to see me pounding the pavement (literally!), or feel the need to catch up on gossip so that after my hour outside, I haven't made it past the second house. Then there's the dog that chases everything that moves, and the shin splints I'll have by next week, the muscle aches, the friction burns on the insides of my thighs . . . You wouldn't happen to have a chocolate bar on you, would you?

Kids. The kids deserve more *quality* time, clean clothes every day, healthy and hearty meals—heck they deserve June Cleaver! I swear I'll be more patient, cut their sandwiches into cute animal shapes, kiss their boo boos, sign all their homework papers so they don't have to miss recess, notice when they are developing and buy the appropriate foundations, compliment them when they accomplish any little thing, think good thoughts always, interrupt my phone conversations to tell them how much I love them . . . But right now I'm a little sleepy . . . I just need a few minutes . . . I'll start after my nap . . . .

This is just the tip of this resolution iceberg and the excuses for failure can take many forms. The truth is that resolutions are short lived (without the aid of electrical shock therapy!) and we all prefer hanging out in familiar territory. All the self-help books, advice columns, and "tell it like it is" assistance work until regular life resumes. When you're not looking, it's so easy to slide back into old habits. But don't beat yourself up—I don't. I'll probably make the same resolutions next year. I may even make it to Valentine's Day before they are history. I could get lucky this year. Anything's possible . . . Anyone see my list? I could have sworn it was right here a minute ago.

Tricks and Treats

Halloween is (by far!) my favorite "mini" holiday. I can only remember being a clown one year. (My costume was puce and yellow. *Puce.* I was hooked on the word *puce* from that day forward.) Then I do believe I was a "hobo" every other year until I outgrew "Trick or Treat." Almost everybody gave the usual junky candies, some evidently saved from previous years, and a few gave regular-sized bars. One family always gave a can of soda, and the best was the old man who gave everyone fifty cents, every year! That was a fortune in those days. (Hint: Elvis hadn't been drafted into the army yet.) You could even go back to his house more than once since he drank a couple of six-packs while he waited for kids to ring the bell. Then there was Old Sophie, the one trick we had to endure each year. She threw ladles of water on us but we weren't surprised—she was mean every day. Mrs. Stephens, on the other hand, whose house looked like something from *House On Haunted Hill*, dark and spooky, would invite us in and bring us straight to her dining room where there was a treat feast waiting on her big dining room table. We could stay as long as we liked, have apple cider and a spice bar, and then put anything we wanted into our bag. Most things were squishy, like soft cookies, so we would save her until last, so we could hand carry the goods home to our waiting parents. They would eat all the things she made, saying that they wanted to "test" them to make sure there wasn't anything harmful in there. Ha! We only fell for that one a couple of times. And it was Mrs. Stephens who planted the love for Halloween in my little hobo soul.

As soon as I was married and we had our first baby, my Halloween gene kicked in. I don't believe in the pagan part of it, and I certainly don't understand the big uproar over it; it's just a fun day for kids to dress up. Unfortunately, my kids weren't as enthusiastic about wearing their costumes as I was about designing and sewing them. For the bicentennial, I made Pilgrim costumes. The kids won first prize for the "cute" category in school and it was a wonderful day. The next year came a chicken costume, a dinosaur, Little Bo Peep (out of my sister's wedding dress) and, again, we won in appropriate categories. Mothers started having closed meetings about how to have me snuffed out since they were into paperbag costumes and store-bought masks. But it was so much fun! The next year I made a Big Mac costume, a large order of fries costume to go with it, a can of Coke costume, and a three-layered ice cream cone costume. I was constantly dieting and for some reason the kids always ended up wearing food costumes. How Freudian! Then it was my two-layered strawberry shortcake costume that collapsed when you sat down (an engineering marvel!), my Geisha girl costume, and a King Henry costume (complete with a turkey leg that I had to varnish after dogs began to chase my little Henry). By this time, I was as unpopular as could be with the other mothers, but it didn't matter—nothing would stop me now. Poodle skirts, fairy princesses, animals of all sorts, mimes, Scottish laddies, nurses, BIC lighters and yes, even dueling Elvises (or is it Elvii?) sprang from my sewing machine. But I was generous, loaning out my costumes to anyone who asked. After all, it's the spirit of the day that matters, right? Well, the party poopers who were most offended by my costume efforts got together to decide what to do about it, and my darkest day occurred when they stopped not just the judging of costumes but also allowing them to wear them at all. In fact, that's just about when that whole pagan thing got started and it makes me wonder . . . was it a plot? I suppose it was less messy than having a hit put out on me. We had no choice but to move to another town!

My kids don't dress up much anymore but I still do. When the neighborhood kids stop by, there are all kinds of fun things in store. Of course I dress up—but not scary. I have been known to answer the door in my yellow leotard and tutu (in my size it's more like a tutu by four-four!), my fifties outfit, even the nun's habit if I'm feeling particularly charitable. They get their candy, and much more. We play music all night, give away bonus prizes, allow the little ones to experience a two-fisted money grab (it's a shopping experience deluxe!). I realize I'm having way more fun than the kids but the good news is that we moved to a town where almost everyone joins in on the festivities. People have spook houses in their own homes and decorate their yards like cemeteries with funny gravestones. I have to borrow my grandkids to take part, but it's worth driving hundreds of miles to get them. In our subdivision, they bring your treats to you if you don't make it to their house during regular hours. Talk about service. I can always feel the spirit of Mrs. Stephens looking down on me as I saunter happily among the children, in the knowledge she would be proud of me for carrying on her tradition. The leotard and tutu she's not so sure about, but I get the distinct feeling she thinks I make up for it in pizzazz.

Dysfunction Junction: All Aboard

The Baby

I can die happily now. The baby, fifteen, has finally begun to display some signs of survival skills. Born ten years after the first six, he was viewed by his siblings as the answer to world peace. For years they had begged for another baby and held secret candle-lighting services in the basement in hopes their dream would come true. From the minute they found out about the pregnancy, the whole band of them swung into action to plan his life. They bought clothes, made lists, chose names and each took the time to talk to my midsection, so that the baby would recognize them by their distinct voices. His whole life was planned out, *Lord of the Flies* style, and they considered him their own personal Cabbage Patch Kid.

When he decided to make his entrance, we were caught unprepared. It was Halloween, ten days before my due date, and for the first time none of them had wanted costumes, a shocking development. They were too excited about the baby to even think about dressing up. We had moved to a new house just three months earlier and, of course, I became room mother for my fifth and sixth grade girls when no one else volunteered. The Halloween party was an absolute must and the car was filled with goodies for the festivities. I had frozen plastic spider rings in ice cubes for the punch, cut the tips off black licorice sticks for straws, made cupcakes decorated with bats, goblins and spider webs, and planned games — I was ready. I only knew one other at-home mom and she would take one class and I would manage the other.

Signs of impending labor began that morning at 3:00, but my babies had always taken their sweet time down the birth canal, so I wasn't too concerned. I even shopped for a bathrobe so my backside would be secure on my walks down the hospital halls. The parties started at 1:00 p.m. and I would have plenty of time. Since it was Halloween, I figured my grimaces from any labor pains would be construed as appropriate witch twitches by the children. I had no intention of giving birth there, although the theme of the party would have supported that.

All went well, and during the cleanup process, one of the teachers asked when the baby was due. I replied "today." I mentioned I had been in labor for twelve hours and I'll tell you, if you ever want help cleaning up, use that line as an opener. I was packed and in the car in under five minutes. A call to my husband on the way home, and we were off to experience the birth of our last little bundle of joy.

At the hospital, I felt like I had entered the Twilight Zone. I was hooked up to all kinds of contraptions to monitor everything from my stem to his stern, a first for me. All the others were born during the dark ages — no contraptions. In those days, everyone was surprised, including the doctor, when the baby emerged with the correct number of appendages.

The noise in the room sounded like the undersea world of Jacques Cousteau and as I panted and hissed, my husband, comfortable in a Lazy Boy recliner, ate his way through the goodie bag I had packed (and I emphasize *Lazy Boy*). A look at the clock reminded me that there were still a few hours of Halloween left. I can't have a child on Halloween, no! I can't have a little Boris or Igor. Every birthday party theme will be predetermined and we'll never know who came. Everyone will be in disguise. Stop pushing, I tell myself. Relax. Hold off a little while longer. Tomorrow is All Saints' Day. Saint or goblin, saint or goblin . . . .

The little saint was born just after midnight and we were home in two days. Our oldest was in college and would have to wait until Thanksgiving to meet him. The others, on schedule, took their positions and swept him from our arms. He was, after all, their brother and they assumed all responsibility for his care and feeding. His father and I only caught glimpses of him now and again, and only got to hold him when the diaper was extra diabolical. I felt much like Mia Farrow in *Rosemary's Baby* when the devil came for the baby after its birth. Was I only a vessel for their selfish purposes?

We never thought he would walk or even have any use for his legs. He was carried everywhere like the Pope on his mobile armchair, and with the same amount of pomp. They all had cameras and when we assembled the 660,000 pictures of him into baby albums, his shelf, sagging from the weight, sported as many volumes as our set of encyclopedias. The girls were responsible for bathing, wardrobe and the "cute" factor, and the boys taught him important things like leaning in his high chair to pass gas bubbles. I never had to change his crib sheet—he never slept in there. Each night I would go to his room to admire his growth and he was nowhere to be seen. If I removed him from the clutches of one sibling, another would scoop him up when they heard the rustle of his plastic pants in the crib. His father and I were referees and only called upon to break up fights over who got to hold him or whose turn it was to love him.

Not many kids have eight parents and he could have turned into a real demon. Instead, he was the most loved child in existence and basked in the knowledge that he needed only bat an eyelash and someone would tend to his needs. It was the perfect Stepford scenario—until he learned to say "no."

The girls took him shopping a dozen times a day and the boys thought he was a great "chick magnet" at the theatre and fast food restaurants. Their male friends even asked to rent him to attract females. To curry favor, his siblings made the mistake of promising bonuses if he would go with them and an enterprise was born. In no time, the little scamp knew exactly how to get what he wanted on any given outing. It was genius and his father and I sat back to watch the fun. All he had to do was say "no" and the level of gift enticements was raised to new heights. Come and you'll get two popcorns, sno-caps and a drink. Come and you'll get a Spiderman action figure, a Scooby Doo stuffed animal and I'll bet Mom would let you have a hamster if you wanted. Ha! They might fall for those baby blue eyes, but I had been trained for this. When we put a stop to it before we became the hamster capital of the world, he knew he had met his match. For the first time in his life he became our child, and after several months in a decompression chamber, he appeared almost normal. They still watched over him since we were too old to be trusted. We did the best we could in our advanced state of aging and here we are today, six kids out of college and this man child, ready to embrace the world.

Unfortunately, this world didn't include water, soap or shampoo for his first decade plus. It's funny how they think they can deceive you. Thinking I recently fell off a turnip truck, this prepubescent wonder actually thought I would fall for the running water scam while he sat commode side, chuckling at the genius of this move. A look in the shower stall to see water drops only around the drain gave me the evidence I needed. If an actual body was in the shower, water would have been displaced by his body and would be on the walls also. It was forensic science at its best. Water problem cured, we moved on to the soap issue. A few swabs of the wall for soap residue with the threat of sending them to the FBI lab in Atlanta made him fess up. Now, onto shampoo. Even after a half hour shower and the application of soap, his hair smelled like a stinky dish cloth. Was it too much to expect everything at one time? And should I tell him that deodorant is actually applied after the showering experience, before he puts his shirt on? It seemed possible but hourly reminders were not enough to keep him on track. Then a wonderful thing happened.

Two showers a day, the smell of deodorant everywhere, nails cut, hair fluffed, a smile on his face. The look is unmistakable. There has to be a girl involved somewhere. All the prompting and nagging in the world couldn't do what one phone call from "she's just a friend" accomplished. He actually noticed his hair with the countless cowlicks and requested a styling. Could he buy a new shirt and could he take his "friend" to the show and lunch? And since his wallet was suffering from an inexplicable emptiness, could he borrow some money? Yes, I think he will survive nicely. Now I need this friend to come to the house so a certain someone will notice the condition of his bedroom floor, cluttered with all his clothing and the remnants of his youth. This friend just might be the best thing that happened to both of us. And those same siblings, now much older and wiser (or so they think) have all kinds of advice for him on the lip of his manhood. I think he has taken his share of mental notes on the subject, and with the hygiene part of his program under control, bring on the next test: driving . . . driving? Driving! Nooooo . . . .

Conferences

An IRS audit, root canal, passing a kidney stone—what do all these things have in common? They're all pieces of cake compared to parent/teacher conferences! Your firstborn (by rights) does the sidestroke through your gene pool, gathering the best of traits, accomplishing everything in record time. You smile sweetly as the teacher expounds on things you (as proud parents) are so familiar with you can almost mouth with her. If there is a flaw it is generally in gym and who needs it anyway, right? It's not like "dodgeball" prepares you for anything! You sail out of the room, buttons popping with pride.

The next teacher asks you to actually sit in your child's desk as you confer. You try to wedge yourself in, certain there must be some mistake as wolves must have raised the misguided child who inhabits this desk. There is total chaos within, underneath, all around! You find yourself scrambling to organize the mess as the teacher displays paper after dog-eared paper, crumpled beyond recognition, remarks atop ranging from "Interesting Concept" to "See Me!" You listen in shock as she describes an

"Inspector Gadget" type, his own worst enemy, however intelligent. Dazed, we stagger to the next classroom where I notice that my husband is wearing a hearing-aid device that I didn't notice at first. I wondered why my friends were shouting at us all evening. This teacher (while my husband stares blankly) expresses surprise that he has this disability. Should I tell her that he's actually listening to the Monday night football game and doesn't really care whether our third child plays well with others? I try carrying the parenting ball all by myself as he makes unusual noises at inappropriate times (1st down, perhaps?), leading this poor teacher to believe he has seizures as well as a hearing loss. It must be halftime because he makes eye contact with her before leaving the room.

It is evident that things can't get much worse, but I ask him to sit outside the room if he is going to "act out" as the game excitement escalates. This teacher is concerned that our son has the ability to bring her entire classroom to a halt. What, our happy-go-lucky peacekeeper? When it's time to clean up, if he refuses to end the game early, the rest of the children follow his lead. My own little Napoleon! I can't tell her how happy I am to see this survival tool, however disruptive to her class. I promise her we'll work with him, but it makes me secretly happy to know he has some spunk.

The ink on this teacher's diploma is still dripping as I enter and she hugs me with assurances that if she had a little girl, she would want one just like mine. This is not a morning child and she allows my little darling to pull herself together, seeing the "switch" turn on around 10:00

a.m. when life starts looking pretty good. She notices the unusual snacks she brings which must have a chocolate involvement to even be considered edible. Our work here is not finished but we'll keep this one.

The game is over, the good guys won and Dad says he'll handle the next conference—I can sit it out. He emerges several minutes later with four pages of notes on this tiny preschooler. They are in outline form, with highlights and bullets, and in my wildest dreams I can only see something like the Spanish Inquisition having just taken place. I am still groggy as we head to our last conference.

We have to hear reports from the whole team for our youngest. One of the four asks if we are aware that he has a great deal of trouble handling scissors. Duh! When the fourth child was born and the first three started practicing arts and crafts on his hair, clothing, and skin (and that was just after they tried to cram him down the laundry chute), scissors were removed from the home permanently. They make marvelous wedding gifts. They give us knowing looks, which lead us to believe that this child is the family storyteller. We don't want to know the details. His vocabulary is outstanding—we just pray it is G-rated.

It's over for now. The crazy thing is that we parents are the ones who are actually tested in the conferencing process. I can only imagine the conversations that teachers have when they compare notes. I'd lose television and phone privileges AND be grounded. The good news is that I've got nine weeks to show improvement.

Camp Vacation

When my husband suggested a camping trip with all the kids, it took me by surprise. He never struck me as the outdoor type. I had heard his single childhood account of the Boy Scout Jamboree in Colorado decades ago but those days were long gone and he was happy to have indoor conveniences as close as possible. He was not thrilled to put worms on hooks when the kids tried fishing, choosing the cute little pink eggs instead. His brother had called and asked if we'd like to go with him. This was one of my husband's unmarried brothers and he was accustomed to the quiet bachelor life, eating when he wanted, and doing anything he pleased. I cautioned my husband that it would be quite the rude awakening, literally, if we all went together. He assured me it would be no problem. The kids were used to his bachelor ways.

Away we went, bringing two tents and as much of the house as we could fit in the car. All the way there I preached to the poor creatures. Remember the buddy system—no one goes anywhere alone, not even to the bathroom. The food will be cooked on a grill so don't crab at the black lines across the hot dogs. If you hear animal noises, grab your buddy and run towards the tent. Only drink water from bottles, not the stream. Don't take any chances and let the grown-ups worry about fire. We're going to have so much fun. Oh, and don't take any of Uncle Jim's food. He takes inventory several times a day.

I had packed everyone's grubby clothes, old jackets, holey sweaters, worn out socks and last season's tennies. We wouldn't have to worry if we left something behind. We were camping, not going to a hotel.

Our car followed closely behind my brother-in-law's vehicle. As we exited the freeway, it appeared to be too well-lit for a campsite. Where was the forest? We followed him into the camp entrance. Greeting us was a giant cartoon character statue. There were lights everywhere and a miniature golf course, snack bar, and indoor bathrooms and showers. It looked nicer than any hotel we had stayed at and the kids perked up right away. "Look at the rides and games," they shrieked in unison. "We have to get the tents up before dark," I reminded them, rifling through my purse to see if we could fund this nature experience. We weren't going to get off easy and the chance of a quiet, peaceful weekend looked pretty slim.

We pitched both tents and all eight of us piled into one and Uncle Jim, telling the kids that his snoring would scare bears, took the other. Our tent was as big as a bedroom and we laid out the sleeping bags like spokes so no one would touch anyone else, an often overlooked, very important detail. We positioned ourselves in the middle to referee any squabbles. They were tired enough to fall asleep immediately but I heard Uncle Jim's snoring most of the night and the other campers telling stories and having a good time. The kids got up with the sun but they had to stay quiet since all the other campers had only been asleep for a few hours. They looked like refugees in their old clothes and it wasn't likely we would even see any-thing rustic this weekend. This was no campground — it was a theme park. We had everyone sneak off to the bath-room where Dad was thrilled to sample the hot-water showers. Staying as quiet as our group could, we ate little round donuts and juice and they whispered until about 9:00 a.m. when I broke under the strain and told all of them they could be themselves. By the time Uncle Jim woke up hoping for breakfast, they had finished horse-shoes and shuffleboard and had their eyes on the hayride schedule board. I was hoping they wouldn't notice the signs for the video arcade or the water slide because I had only packed the no-poison-ivy, head-to-toe clothes. It was almost lunch time and we took out the hot dogs and chips. To ward off any mutiny about the black grill marks, I boiled the hot dogs in a pan over the grill. Uncle Jim brought out gourmet submarine sandwiches on real plates with real silverware. Right after lunch he needed to take a nap so we hiked the kids over to civilization to play miniature golf. The only nature we had seen thus far was the gopher trying to eat through my son's sleeping bag to get at the corn chips. With our last few dollars we rented row boats and their father and I pooped ourselves out trying not to bump into each other. We made it back to the tent for supper as Uncle Jim was getting up from his nap.

Our dad was fashioning foil packs, his favorite "when I was a kid" remembrance. You plop your whole dinner in the middle of an aluminum wrapper—entrée, veggies, and dessert—and roll the edges together so it can't escape. Everything cooks at the same time and it's a one-step meal. Uncle Jim brought out steak, tomatoes for slicing, vegetables to butter and cook, and a pie for dessert. Cleanup was a nightmare. The same little gopher from earlier or at least his relatives were very interested in helping us with leftovers. We cleaned up as best we could; everyone made one last trip to the bathroom and we noticed storm clouds rolling our way. We zipped ourselves into the tent and played card games until the first major boomers hit. When the rain started we told the kids we'd be fine but they couldn't touch the roof of the tent or it would leak in on us. There's always at least one scientist in the group who doesn't believe you and we definitely had a few in our tent. First one little poke by Mark, then another, and another, and then it happened. You could see the tent roof sagging under the weight of the water as it pelted down and within minutes the drips began. As they screamed and ran around to escape tiny water drops, they bumped into the walls and water came at us from every angle. Uncle Jim thought we were having fun without him and came to see for himself. One look and he was back in his tent, quiet, comfy, and dry, probably having an after-dessert snack. We fell asleep wet and the next morning we tried to dry off under the hand dryers in the bathroom. Even our clean clothes were wet, so we ate soggy donuts and juice and rolled up the wet tent. Everyone piled in the car; we left a note for Uncle Jim and took off. By the time he woke up, we'd be home, laundry done, tent dried out and all the kids fast asleep. I should live so long. It started to rain but the car roof didn't leak when they poked it, and by the time anyone had to go to the bathroom we were getting out of the car in the driveway. The house was just as we left it. I guess the house elves were busy somewhere else. The kitchen looked the same, only better. I kissed all my appliances, large and small. "I missed you this weekend," I said glancing around the kitchen. Dorothy was right—there's no place like home, there's no place like home.

A Wedding Saga

Author's note: The nature of a saga is long with many twists and turns. This is no different. Get yourself a snack, go potty, put your feet up and hang in there. No apologies for not making a long story short.

A Wedding. What fun. Our first-born child, a daughter, actually brought an unsuspecting gentleman home to meet us, announcing that this was her choice for a life partner. Her father didn't flinch but I could see his knuckles go white and once he released the death grip from the arm chair, he actually shook the hand of the man who would take his own image and likeness away from him. She had brought many boys home before this one, and although we had nothing against the guys themselves, we had one stipulation that none of them could satisfy. In each and every case, she had been attracted to males whose last names sounded like infectious diseases or at best, conditions that needed lancing. And this one was no different in that department but he had come with a bargaining chip. He was over six feet tall and the thought of one of our descendants actually qualifying for a basketball team made her father cave in and give his blessing. We could always hope that this one was a new-age man and would consider taking her last name.

It would be a year before they would tie the knot. Our daughter was living a hundred miles away at the time, he was between jobs, and they could save money if he could live in our house and use her bedroom. We were trying to get rid of kids, not increase our population, but we agreed on one condition: he would be a willing participant in our SILIT program (Son-In-Law In Training). He offered little resistance, which should have been our first clue, and was directed to the room where he would spend the next twelve months, as pink and girly as it could get. He would also share a bathroom with several of his new sisters-in-law-to-be and we knew they would show no mercy for the new trainee. Fighting his way through pantyhose, lotions and sundry girl items, he fell into every trap their female minds could conjure. The boys, on the other hand, were into Olympic horseplay, complete with "wrastling," smelly laundry and enough natural gas to power a small country. As parents, we set the boundaries and they took turns trampling all over them, and him. He was put through the family wringer and he survived, although we must admit he was not valedictorian of his SILIT class of one. He would marry the toughest one we gave birth to and up to this point had showed few signs of the fighting spirit and even fewer survival skills. She was a good foot shorter than he, but we had no doubt about who would kick up the most dust in this relationship. When the time came to begin plans for the nuptials, we showed her the miles of video-tape we had secretly taken during his stay with us, pointed out some trouble spots, like his hesitancy to come when called to dinner. He'd show up to the table, more than fifteen minutes late, and actually expect that there would be something left for him to eat. The table had been picked clean in the first thirty seconds. She insisted that she could handle everything. For his part, he was merely satisfied to graduate from SILIT School and move on to the easier task of marriage. Wedding plans, here we come.

Originally, we planned to take the wedding to Chicago where we had lived most of our collective lives. It would be easier on everyone, except us. But after a few days of making arrangements and faxing more documents than we owned, it became apparent that we would not survive the grueling demands of a long-distance wedding. My older sister Mary Ann called to share an idea that sent us in a totally different direction. Why not take the money we would spend on a fancy hotel wedding, have the house remodeled and after the wedding we would have a beautiful house to show for our efforts? In its simplest form, it sounded like a great idea so Plan B emerged: service in the front yard, reception in the back. The happy couple would stand near the house at the top of the hill for all to witness. We scoped it out and the angle of the yard was too steep to support chairs so we would have to provide roping for the guests to cling to during the ceremony. Even with the bride and groom at the bottom of the hill, the prospect of injury to our guests forced us to come up with Plan C: service at church, reception in the backyard. Our parish, known for its hostile pastor, insulted the happy couple at their first premarital class, so we had no choice but to change parishes. Plan D? To our total joy, the new parish welcomed us with enthusiasm and we were able to put a big check mark and smiley face next to the *Ceremony* category.

Great care was taken to spell everything on the invitations correctly and it was a perfect time to address the name issue. Would our daughter keep her happy, melodious surname or choose a hyphenated combination of the two? Would she ask him to be a man of evolution and take her name? We held it together remarkably well when, in her blind love, she announced she would become Mrs. *his last name.* Our only concern was for her future plans as a doctor and how many potential clients would be skeptical or turn and flee with that name on the door. Information was scrutinized by each household member, the invitations were ordered and everyone took turns licking the envelopes and applying enough postage to settle the national debt. A call to a nearby hotel to secure rooms for the traveling guests seemed easy enough at the time but would prove fruitless as the receptionist had either a spelling or typing disability. When dutiful friends and relatives called, they were told there were no reservations available under either the bride's or groom's family names or any similar names for that date and the hotel canceled everything that had anything to do with names that even resembled ours.

Unaware of the problem at the time, we were on a break-neck pace to get the house ready. When we purchase a home, it's always square footage that appeals to us most, number of bathrooms coming in a close second. The bigger the better, in case something (or in our case *someone*) happens. This house had fourteen different floor coverings on the first floor, wallpaper from the seventies with way too much orange and a kitchen design by Incapacitated R Us. So, in the spirit of the wedding, the decision was made (by me, the children would insist at the child-abuse hearing) to make a few minor changes. "Let's get the wood floors we've always wanted," I hear myself say, a month from the wedding date. I probably should mention that there are ten of us living here at this point and the natives are anything but happy. It seems their sister has other things on her mind and is not doing her *share* and they are sticking pins in a rag doll that resembles her a little too much. While we move the entire first floor to the garage and basement, the happy duo is picking out china, buying a new car and making plans to leave for Alaska the day after the wedding, if they survive the voodoo hex. In spite of the disgruntled mumblings, I still invite several men with various disabilities and multiple bad habits into my home to install my dream floor. They smoke incessantly and at least one of them has a substance abuse problem or at least a muscle disorder. This came to light when we found floor staples imbedded in the walls, ceiling and cabinets. Did I mention that we were not allowed to step anywhere on the whole first floor? That left the ten of us to use one bathroom on the second floor, accessible only by an outside ladder over the balcony. What adventure, I am saying. Isn't this fun? Now and then I catch glimpses of a rag doll that looks a lot too much like me and, come to think of it, I am inexplicably experiencing some pains. In my defense, we did have a bathroom they could have used in the basement, but they were convinced the movie *Child's Play* was filmed down there and the original roll of toilet paper still had the glue attached to the first sheet and it would be that way when we sold the house.

Finally, they could take it no longer. One of the girls had forgotten to bring her climbing clothes after sneaking a shower on the first floor, and was unprepared to scale the ladder in her towel. A family meeting was called at the dining room table (presently in the garage). Complaints were heard, suggestions made, and our third child, a daughter, lamented that the weather looked bad and what happened if it was raining when she was climbing the ladder to her room. "Climb faster," her unsympathetic brothers cried in unison. Two weeks later, we all had more than our share of splinters from imperfect dismounts over the balcony rail, but we had our wood floors, finally! Isn't this grand, I ask and no one seems to hear. Uh-oh . . . the toilets have to be raised now to match the new height of the floors and the wallpaper sure looks dated and the paint looks worn and remember that chandelier I bought at a garage sale that has been hanging from the rafters in the basement for the last five years? Wouldn't it look great in the foyer? Anyone know a good electrician and wouldn't new curtains go great with the new walls? I'm all alone now. Even the dog isn't listening.

The reception in the back yard . . . I love it. My first act was to sacrifice something to the gods for a good weather day. My "thin thighs someday" wish was the best I had to offer — done. Scoping out the backyard, I couldn't help but notice. Where did all those ugly bushes come from and how many yucca plants should one family have? A little landscaping would really make the difference. I'll call someone, heck I could even do this myself. How much? If you do it? Sold! What do you mean the florist can't do the flowers? I can do flowers, no problem. A bridal bouquet, five bridesmaids, boutonnières, a few corsages, church flowers, pew bows . . . music. Music! I need a nap.

The bridesmaids are from all over the continental U.S. and we are making the dresses. One considerate mom says she'll make her daughter's dress if I send the material and pattern. I love that woman. We bought a bolt of garden print material, nothing fancy, nothing that would make noise when you walk or have satellite dishes for sleeves. My super friend, Chris, was on her way from California. She sews like the wind and sings. Hey! She can sing at the church and at the reception. She's Fresno's Karaoke Queen, after all. It's hard to think when you're hungry. Food . . . another concept . . . we can cook everything ourselves. The family's best recipes were collected, reviewed, and under the influence of a few glasses of wine, we decided that we could let go and have it catered. Done. Tents, tables, chairs, and a dance floor were rented, and two porta potties (one pink, one blue) would be nestled behind two very tall bushes to handle the crowd, if necessary. Dresses were under construction, while the bouquets and flower baskets were taking shape in the basement. Centerpieces were designed around little cherubs for the tables. All that remained was the cake, the one thing that could make or break an Italian wedding. For some reason the groom chose this moment to speak and offered to take care of the cake. Not pay for it, mind you, just get one. He had this co-worker who made cakes and she'd be happy to do it. Would this be her gift to them, I ask? Could she send us sample pictures of cakes she had previously baked for weddings? None of my questions or concerns were answered but I dreamed of an authentic Italian cake with sinful fillings, in the knowledge that my Disney-crazed daughter would adorn the top with the Mickey/Minnie wedding statue my sister gave her as a shower gift. Cute, I thought, and one less thing to worry about.

So, if we worked every hour of every day right up to show time, we might have ourselves a wedding. Friends and relatives appeared from nowhere and breathed life and fashion into the house. Far too many items did not make the redecorating cut and were sent to the basement to live out their lives. It looked great. Even the kids were starting to snap back from their zombie modes.

Two days and counting and the roof caved in, literally. But it was only in the basement, thank God. The washing machine overflowed on the first floor and took out the carpeting in the laundry room. I was tearing up the soaking rug as I heard the garbage men come down the street. The caterers were using the garage to cook so there was no hiding place for a smelly pile of rug and padding. With the thrust of Hercules and the speed of Mercury, I ran after the garbage truck with the load, caught them two houses down, threw the mess in the truck, and in my smug satisfaction, skipped back to the house, stumbled into the drainage ditch and twisted both of my ankles. But there was no stopping me now. We were too close. Not even my brother, tearing a muscle no one ever heard of while showing the kids how the big boys play basketball, could slow us down. We got him to the doctor but he was more or less a veggie for the weekend, unable to get out of his jammies for the occasion. When asked who he was, skulking on the sidelines, I told everyone he was the mysterious Guido I referred to so often when I needed to show some Italian muscle. It was perfect.

With an hour to go before the wedding, we were still hemming the dresses of the bridesmaids who had come in from out of town. The bride decided she would, after all, wear a veil so we made it at the last second. She had forgotten shoes so she wore ballet slippers bought by her brothers at Kmart on their way to church. We were a few minutes behind everyone, thank goodness, so we brought the rings and marriage license, both forgotten in the rush. Her dress tore while putting it on, so armed with a needle and thread, we stitched and were ready with minutes to go. I told everyone I had both of my grown sons walk me down the aisle because I couldn't choose between them. The truth was, my ankles were so sore from the drainage ditch incident, I needed both of them to get to my seat. As our daughter came down the aisle, I burst into uncontrollable sobs, surprising myself and everyone else. It wasn't that I was sad to be losing a daughter. It was more like I could finally stop cleaning, fixing, and embellishing. It was the amen moment. The highlight of the service was during the vows when we produced a lace-covered footstool (made by yours truly) so the two of them would be eye to eye. A partnership is a partnership. At the reception . . .

The cake arrived in the back seat of an un-air-conditioned station wagon and had to be reconstructed with towels. I have no idea what it was supposed to look like, but it never did make it into layers. It resembled the Los Angeles Freeway after an earthquake. I cried a second time that day — when the lady handed me the bill for the cake, the one thing the groom was in charge of. Was it too late to take back his SILIT diploma?

A horde of gnats appeared in spite of our repeated applications of bug spray and, of course, it was just as the food was about to be served. God allowed a thirty-second shower to dispel the gnats (do I get a reprieve on the "thin thigh" wish?) and my niece spent a half hour trapped in the porta-potty before she was discovered. Our little guy, four, seized the dance floor in his little white tux and displayed dance moves he did not learn from this family. James Brown would have been proud. When we looked at the photos taken by a team of professionals, everything looked perfect with one exception. This same little guy, the dancing fool, was emulating the groomsmen in all the formal portraits. They had been instructed to fold their hands in front of them, knuckles down, in macho form. No one noticed that he went a step further. He grabbed on to his little male body parts with both hands and hung on for dear life. The photographers never noticed it, they swear.

Well, we did it. And my sister was right. The house looks great. You'd love these floors. We gave the kids gifts for being so tough — gift certificates to our family doctor to have the splinters removed from their inner thighs. It's the least we could do. They kept that rag doll after it was all over and, to this day, every now and again, I still have some inexplicable pains. I wonder . . .

It was a decathlon, after all. We didn't earn any medals for our performance, but we finished the race and that counts for something, doesn't it?

Igloo Country

A trip to Alaska, the Last Great Frontier. We were making plans to visit our married daughter, Jennifer, in Anchorage in March and we didn't want to look like total dummies, so we asked questions. What's the weather like this time of year? That was our dumbest question. They had already suffered about 110 inches of snow and there were no signs of it letting up. For Christmas we all received t-shirts that read "Alaska has four seasons: June, July, August, and Winter." It was suggested that we pack everything we owned warm enough to withstand the bitter cold. Done. Our youngest, Daniel, was five and he would make the trip with his father and me so we had to consider his survival with not a shred of blubber to keep him warm. He was excused from a week of kindergarten *if* he came back with a great report on Alaska to present to his classmates. We hung cameras around our necks and packed notebooks for the cause. We were warned that things were more expensive because everything but snow and ice had to be shipped from the lower forty-eight, so we brought film, snacks, and comfort items with us. No need for sunglasses because of that "six months sun, six months dark" thing and we were in the dark sector of that plan.

We made sure our insurance premiums were up to date and hopped on the plane. One stop in Minneapolis and we could be there in twelve hours. It was a shorter trip to Europe, if I remember correctly, but we did have to go through a bit of Canada so I stopped whining and got into the mood. The people of Anchorage are very festive, and keep their Christmas lights up until mid-March. It looked like Las Vegas as we landed but we later found out that it was the only way to see anything for the six months the light is limited. We arrived in the dark, but I think it was the middle of the day. Actually they leave the Christmas lights up until the Iditarod dogsled race declares a winner. It's as good an excuse as any when things are so bleak for so long.

Leaving the airport, Jenny and her husband raved about the positives of life in the frozen tundra. All I remember is hearing about black ice and how you think it's just wet pavement but you can die at any moment because it's so dangerous. I missed most of the sights because I chose to lie face down on the back seat until we got to the apartment. Or I should say, the shed. It looked like a little storage unit, filled to the brim with all their possessions stacked on top of each other. They had picked up a cat and a dog for company and we heard them scuffling but never caught sight of their actual bodies. We, three weary travelers, checked into a hotel room where the two of them raved about the square footage. Our little one had a look on his face that said, "Save me, Mom," so I stayed near him stroking his little back to allay his fears. I felt him go stiff when Jenny announced that there were some basic survival rules we needed to know before venturing outdoors.

Lesson #1: Moose etiquette. It seems that the moose population in Alaska rivals the squirrel population back home and because they weigh roughly as much as your car, it pays to understand their "ways." Before leaving your house, it is essential to open the door a crack to assess the moose situation. Look left to right. Scan for moose tracks. (Are they all the same size?) If you interfere with a mother moose and baby, you will not live to tell the story. You are stomped to death by the mother before you can get back to the welcome mat. It seems those spindly legs pack quite the wallop. No moose? Sprint to your car and dive into the front seat in case one comes out of the bushes while you are running down the sidewalk. Should you encounter one while driving, know that they have the complete and total right of way. If there is a moose in the right turn lane to the mall, face it; there will be no shopping today, friends. And should you be so unfortunate as to hit one, you had better be prepared. In Alaska, you must take Moose Packing 101 to graduate from high school. You cannot leave a moose down. The meat must be packed by you or I believe you can transfer your rights to a shelter or charitable organization or a crazed person with the Jeffrey Dahmer bone-cutting attachment on his utility knife. Even in the middle of nowhere, like the Iditarod race, if you encounter and kill a moose to save your dogs, you must stop, pack the entire moose and add it to your two-thousand-pound sled, already laden with survival supplies. It's part of the No Moose Left Behind program and they mean business. It takes an average person four days to pack a moose — body, hooves and antlers — so unless you want to use your vacation time in this pursuit, it's better to avoid situations where a moose might present itself.

Lesson #2: Glaciers. The rule here is, don't eat blue snow. We arrived at the end of the Snow Sculpture Festival, minutes before the start of the Ice Sculpture Festival, followed closely by the I'm Tired of Sculptures Festival. To get away from all the excitement, we were driven to the Portage Glacier to see nature's ice sculptures. It's true. The ice is blue. My husband positioned our son on the glacier and took pictures of his terrorized little body atop very blue ice. "You want him to get an A on his report, don't you?" he snapped when I asked if it wasn't a bit too dangerous. "The ice is melting at record speed and it's anyone's guess when this place will be a swamp," I huffed over my left shoulder. I was still miffed that the museum was closed for the day and I would not get to see the acclaimed "Voices from the Ice" narrative I was promised. As a consolation, I was guided to the gift shop and encouraged to purchase a brooch the size of my foot, carved from legally mined, ancient, authentic walrus tusk. I would regret this purchase later as we had to pay for overweight luggage on the return trip.

Lesson #3: Avalanches. In this state, if there isn't an avalanche, something is wrong and they cause one with explosive devices. There are little flags everywhere outside the city marking the danger zones and you'd better not mistake them for ski resorts, or bad things happen and you are on the eleven o'clock news if nothing more disastrous preempts you.

Lesson #4: Food. It's the *don't ask don't tell* world of road kill soufflé, something or other sausage and we think they're not poisonous berry desserts. Most everything smelled like the beast had only too recently been relieved of its skin for our tasting pleasure and trying the appetizers was like a foray into Wild Kingdom. The alternative to mystery meat would have been salad but we did not bring enough money. Since the growing season is approximately four days long, every single salad ingredient is considered not native to the area and we had to pay shipping charges and import taxes every time we ordered one.

We couldn't stand any more lessons, so we decided to live dangerously and enjoy ourselves. We shopped for souvenirs and bought back scratchers from moose antlers. Did you know that a moose loses its antlers every single year right after mating season and has to start over? Bummer. That leaves a lot of antlers lying around for crafty Eskimos to buff or carve. Oh, for the boys we bought Ulu knives and we couldn't resist some of those gold-covered moose doodles in gift boxes. It's the perfect holiday housewarming gift. The girls fared a little better with nesting dolls and beaded purses but our little one got the best gift of all. The state bird of Alaska is the puffin, which looks like a cross between a penguin and a toucan. Jenny bought him a puffin hat that looks like it's nesting on your head with its feet coming down over your ears.

He wore it for the next several years religiously until misguided kids started making fun of it and trying to pull off the cute little webbed feet.

We did notice one thing. We were picked up in a brown car that we swore was blue when it left the continental U.S. All the other cars were brown, too. Salt and cinders are not in the Anchorage budget so they throw sand and dirt down on the ice. A typical car wash cost ten dollars and we were informed that it usually took several times through to get to the original paint color. The residents accept that their cars will return to their normal color after the last snow fall, or Memorial Day, whichever comes first.

We all made it back alive and our little guy got an A+ on his Alaskan report. He used a pointer while showing his slides and just to make sure everyone got in the mood, we served Klondike bars for ambience during the presentation. We videotaped every adorable minute of the report with pride to be cherished forever, or at least until his big sister taped right over it with the Conan O'Brien episode spoofing the ordeals of choosing the perfect "boy band" members. So, I had no choice but to put the photo album with the three thousand pictures of Alaskan scenery in the safe deposit box right next to the scissors he'll get when he turns twenty-one.

Grooming Mishaps

Most of my friends look like they just stepped out of a salon, no matter what time of day it is. I am suspicious of them. Do they have a hidden someone who tends to them behind the scenes? Do they have help wrestling the kids in the morning, getting them bathed, fed, and dressed like they're bound for egg rolling at the White House? And how do their husbands leave every morning with starched shirts, pants with the correct number of pleats down the front, and most shocking of all, matched socks! I can't remember a time when I felt that *together*.

Growing up in a large family where bathroom time was at a premium, we all learned how to barter and connive for a few precious moments alone. You always have the person who takes the forty-gallon shower, using all the hot water available. He has no regard for the rest of the family and forces the remaining group to choose between an eye-opening frigid shower, dabbing the offending parts with a damp washcloth from the kitchen sink, or just going dirty. You make the choice to (a) get up earlier tomorrow, (b) trade your allowance to the hot water pig so you can, in turn, be the hated family member, or (c) spray enough cologne on yourself so no one suspects you have a problem. And mirror time was unheard of. For the first decade of my life, I thought I was a direct descendant of Abraham Lincoln, having to use my reflected image in the toaster or soup spoons to catch a glimpse of my hairdo or check for French toast in my teeth. There was no choice but to adapt to the circumstances and use my allotted thirty seconds well.

College was no better. There were ten sinks, six shower stalls, and one bathtub. But there were forty-two girls sharing the limited space, some of whom had trained at military school, sported sharp elbows and used threatening glances that would cause a military battalion to retreat. Again adapting, my washcloth was my salvation, and a quick look into my stapler at my reflection each day led me to believe that all was well. (Although I wondered why Lyle Lovett was looking back at me.)

Married life was not the time to begin fussing. My husband and I met at a picnic. I had taken little care that day to primp. The rolls from my curlers were still tight when I realized I had also forgotten shoes, so I would have to play the inevitable picnic games barefooted. He didn't seem to notice any deficiencies (that day, anyhow) so two years later, we united. It probably helped that he had nine brothers and sisters and they had the same bathroom problems we did. He seemed okay with my plain-Jane style so the need to change seemed unnecessarily silly. No need to frighten him with the morning shock of the *without makeup* me.

Kids came at a furious pace and what little bathroom time I had enjoyed was cut to almost nonexistence. Personal time, that is. I no longer have any memories of being alone in the bathroom. It was the gathering place, a time for family discussions. Of course, they were helpful. They would hand me toilet paper just at the right time and once I unwound it from the other bathroom fixtures, it was mine to employ as I saw fit. I never had to worry about flushing. It was taken care of by the "Helper of the Day."

Something they learned at school, the helper was the line leader, organizer, weather forecaster; in short, the answer person. They would decide (in secret meetings held hours before I awoke) who the helper for that day was and that was that. They could be all over the house, playing and having fun and as soon as I got within ten feet of the bathroom door, they would form a cluster like confused sheep and enter en masse for the festivities. At bath time, I bathed the six of them all at once, lined up oldest to youngest, shampooing, soaping, and rinsing in one sweeping motion. It still took most of the hot water and by the time it was hot again, my husband was in, showering off the day's troubles. I would collapse into bed and my dreams would be filled with waterfalls, spas, and swimming pools glistening in the sunlight. It was the closest I would get to water that day. Getting up before the crack of dawn was not the answer, either. The kids would hear the faucet turn and be assembled in an instant. While I was scooting them to the kitchen, hoping to get them interested in cereal and juice, my dearly beloved would jump back into the shower. He never moved in his sleep and the sheets were relatively clean. What could possibly happen in those few hours of slumber to warrant another shower? It didn't matter. Hot water gone, I spritzed myself with the kitchen hose and longed for the time when I could have a quiet, hot bath — ALONE. I still cry when I think of the day it happened. I filled the tub with ALL the hot water and explained to the children that Mommy needed a few minutes to take a bath and they could watch TV. Thinking back, I should have locked the door, but I was so confident that it would work that I actually left it ajar. I filled little cups with fried cheese doodles for them to snack on while they watched Mister Rogers at the Crayola Factory.

A few minutes into my glorious moment, I heard a little knock on the door.

"I'll be out in just a few minutes" I sang cheerily.

"But, Mommy, I have to tell you something," was the reply.

"Can it wait for Mommy to finish her bath?" I asked, my mother antennae rising.

"No, I have to tell you right away."

Against my better judgment, I allowed her to enter my *sanctum sanctorum*. We had lovingly nicknamed her, our third child, SBD (Silent But Deadly). She was so soft-spoken but oh so cunning. I couldn't hear what she was saying so I beckoned her closer.

"Honey, tell Mommy what's wrong." I should have seen it coming but as she leaned over to whisper in my ear, her cup of cheese doodles toppled into the bath water, creating an orange slick that attached itself to my flesh in an instant. Horrified, she ran from the room without telling me her important "something," and equally horrified, I realized that I was sitting in the last of the hot water. As I stood up and rinsed the orange coating from my body with freezing water, I lifted my eyes heavenward: "I give up, God. I will NEVER be so foolish. It was so selfish of me. I promise I will NEVER abuse water, time or motherhood ever again!"

A promise is a promise. Especially to God. He's got some great deterrents that help keep me in line, like lightning and pestilence. I've lowered my standards considerably and I tell my children to this day what I told them then: "Don't worry about how you look or what you wear or how you smell. It's your personalities that people will remember. But just in case, don't get too near anybody and stand under ceiling fans if at all possible." The Child Abuse Hotline hadn't been invented back then, so they just disappeared to their rooms and made journal entries for their future *Mommie Dearest* tell alls. We've got a nest egg set aside for therapy in case any of them hasn't recovered from their spartan upbringing (that's because the Child Abuse Hotline DOES exist now and our lawyer recommended that we cover all our bases in case poor parenting is retroactive).

It occurs to me that things might have been different if our family even remotely resembled any of my friends' families. Most of them have the 2.4 children the "norm" allows. It's entirely possible that they don't have any of the problems that plague this large group. We've replaced four water heaters in the last ten years, not to mention our

120

washer, dryer, and stove. We're looking into industrial-grade appliances and my dream continues for the perfect refrigerator: One with two glass doors like in a deli. Spy what you want and in one fell swoop, open the door, extract the desired item and whip that baby closed before any cold escapes.

We strive for the good life but it's different for every family. There are few families like ours, where crowd control and swat team ethics are the ruling force. When we exit our home, the neighbors get a special viewing treat. Unlike their happy, organized, squeaky-clean image, we produce our own special brand of fashion: static cling. Add to that the wild shouts of "I call Shotgun!" and "Don't make me sit next to her. I had to sit next to her last time" and you get the picture. My husband and I make eye contact. He squeezes my hand and says, "It won't be long until they're all gone and we'll miss these moments." I'm looking into the eyes of a man I thought I knew. It's worse than I thought. He's given up the fight and is merely gliding to the finish line. It's true then. They got to him. I'll have to carry the ball all alone. I should have bought that pillow I saw in a magazine—I Work Alone Without A Net. I could go to my room and squeeze it until the stuffing popped out. I feel better already.

Shhhhhhhhhhhhh . . .

Family traditions at Christmas make the hustle and bustle of the season worth the trouble. We're lucky that most of the kids make the effort to get here and we have ourselves a ball while everyone is together. My son Mark is renowned for his childlike holiday spirit and over the years has played many holiday roles. His Happy the Elf costume has seen many years of wear as he was always one of Santa's helpers at the nursing home his friend's family owned. He'd jump around as elves are wont to do and would even appear, if coerced, at his little brother's day care while his big brother, Joe, played the role of Santa. They were a good team. One year a problem arose at the nursing home. The guy who played Mrs. Santa had grown a beard and mustache over the year and the residents were bothered that Mrs. Claus had let herself go to that extent. Unwilling to shave for the occasion, there was no choice but to promote Happy to the Mrs. Claus role. The problem was that there was only one Mrs. Claus costume to be rented in the whole town and if you didn't get it first, you were out of luck. He called to lament that this year someone else got the dress and his debut as Mrs. Claus would be a no-go without a dress. "No problem. I'll make you one," I heard myself say.

At Thanksgiving, I took all the necessary measurements and set myself to the task. Mark had played football through college and is not your basic sissy type. I had to add many inches to the largest pattern and I used a stretchy material also, just in case. There he was, clad in red velvet, huge tennis shoes showing, twirling as I pinned the hem on his fur-trimmed dress. In case he had an opportunity to travel as Mrs. Claus, I included an apron, cape and hat with his wig, gloves and granny glasses. A mother could not have been more proud.

He took over the job as Santa for the little ones in our home, too. We'd wait until all the packages were opened and he'd sneak into the bathroom and pull the suit out from under the sink. He'd slip out the back door and head down the street with his sleigh bells ringing, waving to all the kids as he left for his next stop. He was always sleep-deprived and too tired to enjoy the day because each year he arrived ultra-early on Christmas morning and would have only an hour or two of sleep before duty called. One year he expressed the desire to get the Santa thing out of the way and get a few good hours of sleep. I had him get dressed, handed him the bag, and went to give the kids the great news. I had discovered Santa in the house putting presents under the tree and if we were really quiet, I thought we could spy on him without making him mad. We really had to be quiet, though. You wouldn't want to get Santa mad this close to present time. All of us snuck down the hall to the second-floor railing, and there he was, Santa! He was busy reading the note they left for him, nibbling on a cookie and attempting to sip some milk through his heavy beard. Their eyes were the size of saucers and they couldn't believe their good fortune. Santa, right in Grandma's house. He finished putting all the gifts around the tree and sat down to write a response to the note they had left him. A red sharpie had been left for this purpose and he picked it up, used it and laid it back down. As he was getting up to leave, he picked up the baggie of carrots for the reindeer and as he twirled around, caught sight of his speechless admirers. He put his finger up to his lips to ensure their silence, and then lifted the carrots with a big "thumbs up" thank you gesture on behalf of the reindeer. With the bag over his shoulder he left, his bells jingling softly. With a, "Ho Ho Ho, Merry Christmas," he was gone.

Stunned by the miracle they had just witnessed, it was our oldest granddaughter, Killian, who finally managed to speak. "Grandma, he left his pen. His pen! Can I have it? Please?" "Sure. You'll get a pretty penny for that on eBay. You're one lucky girl. Go put it in your suitcase, quick." Then it hit her. "Aw, shucks. I wanted to see the reindeer. Do you think he's still on the roof?" I assured her that he was probably in Muscatine, Iowa by now but I gathered all of the little ones to read his letter to them: "Dear Children, Thank you for the milk and cookies. They were the best cookies I have had so far tonight. And the reindeer will be so glad you remembered them with the carrots. Please be good all year so I can come back again next year. Thanks. Your friend, Santa." They were so excited but they chided their uncle when he came out of the bathroom: "I don't know how you always miss him every year. You really have bad luck." "I know," he told them. "But I wasn't a very good boy this year and I didn't want him to forget you," he said and they bought it. No one can convince these kids that Santa doesn't exist. They saw him with their own eyes. I know I believed it. Santa earned an Academy Award that night. It was unanimous. Not a dry eye in the house.

Home Is Where Your Laundry Lives

House History

We have friends who have lived in the same house since they were born. As soon as the opportunity arose, they purchased it from their parents, who headed straight for Florida or a fancy retirement community. The parents were aware that the roof was minutes away from disintegrating, the water heater was held together with duct tape, and the air conditioner was making noises like it was digesting a flock of geese. The front stairs were rotting away from the porch and the windows wouldn't open more than three inches from warped wood. The new homeowners were giddy with excitement at the thought of keeping the family home in the family. It was at approximately this same moment that an unusually fertile mother termite laid eggs that would produce an alarming swarm of termites near the home's foundation. People call these types of homes "money pits" but the people at Home Depot will come to know and love them and count on them for year-end profits.

We were in that category for a short time. We had no choice but to buy unworthy homes, as long as they were big and could support our numbers. Weekends were spent fixing them up until they would be just as we hoped. We'd get transferred about two weeks later, move and start the process all over again.

Our first house was a rental and one of the first prefabricated ones I had ever seen. My husband and his roommate had lived there for a year before we were married and we spent three years trying to get used to it. The walls were so thin I had to beg him to wait until he was in the car and down the driveway before he blew his nose, so he wouldn't wake the kids. It was right next to a Laundromat and people kept ringing the doorbell to see if we had change for the dryers.

Our second home was a palace by comparison. It was a Cape Cod style, only a block from the first house and had a big yard. It was there I grew my first eggplant and watermelon. Every day I went out to water the garden and I would turn the eggplant and watermelon so they wouldn't have a bad side. When it came time to pick them, I didn't have the heart to eat them, so we shellacked them and used them for table decorations. The zucchini was another story. It would be the size of a hot dog one day and a Louisville Slugger the next. It frightened us enough to keep the children out of the garden just in case a zucchini mutiny broke out. Right in the middle of loving this house, we got an opportunity to move back near both sets of parents and many of our siblings, and we did it so the kids could see relatives more often.

This home was in a suburb of Chicago and considered a bungalow by Windy City standards. We stripped wood, broke out walls, finished the attic for more bedrooms, purchased new storm windows and attached a new porch. We lived minutes from my in-laws and only a few feet from the fire house. Every time the fire alarm went off, my phone would ring. "It's not us," I would assure my mother-in-law. She was always embarrassed but she'd say, "I was just calling to check on the kids." If I did not answer the phone when she and my mother called daily, the National Guard was alerted and the hunt for us would begin. We lived there for ten years and had six little ones by the time we moved to Fresno, California.

Now this was a house: five bedrooms, three bathrooms, a family room, and a swimming pool. We really didn't need the house. The kids swam summers from 8:00 a.m. to 10:00 p.m., and on school days every second they could. We had lemon, orange, grapefruit and apricot trees, a grape arbor and strawberries from February to October. Our azaleas looked like trees and the mountains and Sequoia National Park were less than an hour away. We did the dance of joy in our first master bathroom. No more waiting our turn! This place was close to heaven and we enjoyed it three years to the day. Back to Chicago, the suburbs, and family.

Looking for a house here was more complicated. At least three hundred new subdivisions had gone up since we last visited and it was too confusing. Most of the new subdivisions had English names, like Bristol, Birmingham, and Devonshire. I guess they thought they could tack on a few thousand dollars more if the name sounded more sophisticated. After weeks of horror after household horror of crooked walls, leaking basements, and sinking foundations we opted for a tried and true pre-owned home.

We found a six-bedroom colonial with a fenced-in backyard and a screened-in porch, a first for us: kind of outdoors without the bugs. We were promised when we moved there that the company that brought us from California was here to stay. They had been bought out by a St. Louis company but we would NOT have to move. Before we chipped the cork board off the boys' walls we were putting the house up for sale and heading to St. Louis. Did I mention I was pregnant?

In my second trimester we said goodbye to our neighbors and headed to our new home. Five kids were in braces by then and we had to change doctors, dentists, everything for this move. The house we found was the same price as the one we left but looked like a castle, the only good thing about leaving the Chicago area. Prices were much better in St. Louis and we got a Tudor-style house with a two-story limestone entry turret. For the next ten years we would have more fun here than we could have imagined. The yard was perfect for parties, egg hunts, weddings, you name it. The highlight for my husband was the four-car garage. We were able to hide everything we owned in there and still park three cars! It was hard to say good bye to the "castle" but a new job took us to a suburb of Indianapolis, a short four hour-drive away.

My husband didn't even wait for the realtor to slow down before he jumped out of her car to look at our next house. It was everything he loved with three fireplaces as a bonus. The rooms were huge and all our little guy said before we left was, "Make sure I get a red room." Here it was, his red room! And while it was an absolutely fabulous home, I couldn't wait to ask about the little sign hanging from the big "For Sale" sign. "What does 'deeded boat dock' mean?" Although we were one house away from actually having lakefront property, we could get a boat. A boat! And it just so happened that our neighbors in St. Louis were upgrading and were selling their nineteen-foot boat, in good as new condition. I was shocked when the skipper said we could buy it and I bought a trailer hitch that day. The water where we would dock the boat was just the perfect size for beginners. It was only eighteen-hundred-acres in size but because it was a reservoir, there were many tricky spots where trees and home foundations still lived. Six propellers later, I got the hang of things and with my boating safety course under my belt, each trip out became more fun, less treacherous. It was four years of great adventure.

This latest home cannot be described properly. Everyone says, "You have a beautiful home," and I always add, "It would be much nicer if I didn't live in it," because a house is a house. We have six bedrooms here and six bathrooms. Can you believe it! I finally get the house I needed twenty years ago. But it's great for visitors and for family during the holidays. There's a little stream out back but the boat is in dry dock. This should be our last house before retirement and my husband always asks where I would like to live. Although I would like to be near water, I don't think it really matters. My dream home would be to take something from each of the other houses. It's the people I enjoyed most. I have never lived anywhere that I haven't met the most amazing friends. So, if I was being honest, I'd like a house with a lot of houses around it where all my friends could come and live, too. But then again, I think I could live on a raft or in an igloo, as long as they had phone service, and maybe plumbing. Yes, plumbing would be the hook, phone service and plumbing. I could live anywhere.

P.S. In case the moving gods are listening, I didn't really mean it. I like it where I am. Please don't make me move all this stuff again . . . please . . . I was just kidding . . . please.

Bargain Basement

You can find just about anything you'd ever want or need in my basement. I'm not kidding. To the untrained eye, it looks like a tornado-riddled aftermath, but to the astute crafter, it's an answer to life's dream. Throwing things out never makes any sense. You always need the exact item an hour after the garbage men have thrown it on the truck and you end up buying everything twice. So if you never throw anything away and you have enough plastic containers and an exceptionally large storage area, it makes perfect sense to hang onto every little scrap, just in case. Here are some of the invaluable things that have come out of the basement:

Enormous cactus plant: artificial, of course. Dad kept killing the real ones at his office so we located a clay pot, some wooden dowels, green corduroy fabric and some sour gum tree balls (in the appropriate areas in the gardening, workbench, sewing and natural & dried flower sections), and the kids and I built a giant cactus he couldn't kill. We gave it to him for Father's Day. It never made it to his office and we actually believed him when he said it fell off the luggage rack on top of the car on his way to work.

Trees: We have eleven Christmas trees, fully decorated, waiting for the season or a Christmas in July moment. Our holiday supply area grows each year and threatens the other sectors, but if someone is having a play and needs props, they know where to come. The best tree in the basement, made by a creative friend, is a his/her tree, inspired by Bob and Delores Hope. It seems they had differing ideas and battled over the style of their Christmas tree. Their savvy designer solved the problem by putting the tree on a revolving stand. Ours is similar as one side is Victorian and feminine and the other side is masculine and den worthy. It rotates so that both of us can have the tree we want at least half the time when we're together and it can be stopped so that when I'm alone I can enjoy my delicate tree. We have a tree with the state quarters in it, three with the first Christmas participants aboard, two with birds' nests, pine cones and other natural fauna and flora imbedded, and several for the young at heart. At holiday time there's a tree for everyone's room as well as several extra for the gobs of gifts that end up under them for Christmas morning. They're pre-lit, of course, and make spectacular night lights.

We have life-size stuffed witches, a snowman family, several light-up pumpkins, and enough Mardi Gras beads and masks to rival New Orleans. There are flowers everywhere, enough silk to start my own shop, ribbons of every color and size, dowels, craft paints, buttons, glue and all the binding wire you'd ever need. Two tables are necessary to house the leftover accessories from previous homes that don't "go" with the new house. In our family, someone is always moving or there's always those pesky "projects" for school. Just the other day, my friend Jen called to lament that her son had to give a presentation on a Chicago gangster and needed a fedora. My immediate response was "What color? We have black, brown, and grey." The same child had needed a '70s outfit for spirit week and his first question was, "Mom, do you think Mrs. Fel (my nickname) would have something?" A quick trip to the hanging rack and he was styling a la Greg Brady in his dapper leisure suit. If I don't have it, there's material and six sewing and embroidery machines that can help whip up what you need in hours.

Scrapbooking supplies: Don't even go there. When do you do most of your creative work? After the kids have gone to bed, the dishes are done, and the laundry is caught up. When do the stores close? Long before that, so you simply must have what you and everybody else might need at hand, in every color and every style, just in case. There's a table and chairs ready for a workshop, if one breaks out.

Baskets: Every shape and size is available for any occasion, any time, any place. They can't be too big or too small and there's a pile of tissue paper nearby in the wrapping paper section that can convert any basket to the exact specifications needed.

Pizza/Baking supplies: A must. We have boxes, medium and large, cardboard circles to match, Barbie tables and insulated bags for hot and fresh delivery. There are industrial-sized cans of pizza sauce for larger projects like football teams, student council gatherings, you know, just in case. My personal limit was 107 pizzas one night for our son's college football team. That's a whole different story. Next to the pizza supplies are all the copper and metal Martha Stewart cookie cutters and kits we use for baby showers, weddings, holidays, and just because. I love that girl. She saves things, too—and shellacs them! You gotta love that.

Baby clothing and toys: Our daughter gives away or sells everything as the kids outgrow them and there's nothing to pass on, for tradition. I complained. She didn't have the storage space so now everything is living in my basement in scores of plastic tubs. Taking the baby's picture in the same outfit her big sister wore at the same age makes me very happy, so there. And you never know when a baby will break out in this family. We're ready with bottles, bouncers, buggies, strollers, cribs and mobiles. Twenty-four hours notice and we're ready to roll.

Costumes: There are tubs and more tubs and even two hanging racks of costumes spanning the last thirty years. There's the traditional Mr. & Mrs. Santa Claus costumes, Happy the Elf, Easter bunny costumes in all sizes, and an adult-sized chick hatching from an egg costume, just in case. We have dueling Elvis costumes, two peas in a pod costumes, '50s skirts with saddle shoes, nine nun's habits we used for The Holy Rollers volleyball team, and even a knight in shining armor costume. Just in case. My French fry costume, made in 1979, still gets the kids free food if they wear it into any fast food restaurant, especially when accompanied by my cheeseburger costume, complete with French knots for sesame seeds. I made boxes from poster board for McDonald's and Burger King, and with the drink cup costume the whole family eats for free. We have a three-layered ice cream cone costume (the food theme was big as I have dieted most of my married life); Little Bo Peep out of my sister's wedding dress, complete with staff and lamb; and an engineering feat in a two-layered Strawberry Short Cake that collapses when you sit down and pops back up when you stand. My chicken costume was a designing coup and with minor adjustments, My King Henry costume was a show stopper. We had to varnish the turkey leg after our little King was chased by several neighborhood dogs.

There's still room for a few more things but with the big screen TV, the couch and foosball table, our basement serves our family and the neighborhood quite nicely. We have separated the civilized part from what they call my "jungle." Only my best friends with impeccable medical histories are allowed down there. It is not for the weak or meek. We've only misplaced a couple of people in the past years but, in our defense, we do have a fully stocked refrigerator down there and a convenient, functioning bathroom. We have posted signs all the way down the stairs like "The End Is Near" and "Have Your Insurance Premiums Been Paid?" and the popular "Last Chance To Turn Back." Some people just like to live on the edge. For me, it's an escape. I slip away and through the registers I can hear them asking, "Where's MOM?"

"I don't know but her car's here."

"Oh, I'll bet she's in the basement. You go down."

"No, you go down."

"I asked you first."

"I asked you louder."

"I dare you."

"I double dare you."

Then, from the top of the stairs, "Mooooom, you down there?" I never answer. There are just enough dark corners to keep them upstairs and if I make a few noises when they open the door, I'm home-free for days. Life is good.

Science Project

What will you be remembered for when you depart this earth? I've given a great deal of thought to the legacy I will leave behind. Will it be the countless hours of community service, the thousands of committees helped with my fundraising efforts, the loads of costumes created for school projects and church pageants, the tons of pizzas hand-tossed and donated to various groups, or even the seven children I raised? I picture the ceremonies that might take place, decades from now, highlighting the crowning achievements of my life, with my aged husband being helped to his feet by my adoring children and their families, all present to bask in the glow of their mother/wife/grandmother's accomplishments. When the award is announced, however, I can see the stunned reaction of my family and the entire crowd gathered. "What did they say?" asks my husband who has refused to get a hearing aid for the past thirty years despite our hoarse voices shouting encouragement to make the choice. "Science? They're giving her an award for scientific achievement? This, the woman who, as a teen, helped release the frogs (half-frozen in the lab freezer) that hopped stiffly from the biology lab to short-lived freedom in the teachers' lounge? The same woman who tried to give the fetal pig a second chance by administering CPR? Maybe I *should* go in for that hearing test." I can see the looks on my children's' faces go from puzzled to knowing as they clarify the award.

It seems that during my lifetime I was able to supply more science projects from our home refrigerator (and the bread box) than any other single person in the continental United States. The slide show begins. It highlights slime and mold figures, spanning the animal, vegetable, and mineral categories. Notably among the hundreds of slides are baked potatoes resembling Tom Hanks in *Castaway* (before he shaved, of course) Jell-Os depicting battle scenes from the Civil War, and (I am proud to see) a green bean casserole of the Last Supper with only a few Apostles missing. I get misty as parents fling themselves across their children's laps and cover their eyes to prevent them from seeing the horror.

In my defense, I tried to keep up with the food problem. If you have kids, you know that if they eat the same thing twice within a three-month period, they are scarred for life. Their grades drop dramatically and they start hearing voices. Trying to measure the EXACT amount they would eat on any given evening was the fine line I could never walk. Thus, leftovers were born (and ultimately raised) in our home. The daughter of a mother who survived the Depression, I was taught *NEVER* to waste and heaven help us if we ever threw anything out. My siblings and I offered to mail several meals to the starving children in China and we always paid for our insolence in our rooms or on a chair, staring at the corner of a wall. When we emerged, the offending leftover was waiting on our plate and sooner or later (keeping it in your cheeks only works for squirrels) we swallowed it.

Still, and after years of adult therapy, I was sure my leftovers were different, better than anyone's. I imagined my children skipping home from school, throwing kisses to the crossing guard, and knocking each other down to be the first inside to savor last night's delights as their after-school snack. Imagine my surprise when they attacked the Ding Dongs, Oreos, Nutter Butters, Jell-O, anything and everything but my tasty leftover supremes. Undaunted, I organized a group of neighborhood moms and we traded leftovers in the hopes that the kids would not catch on and we could perpetrate this worthwhile endeavor. Under the cover of darkness, mothers of the neighborhood (children safely tucked in bed) would gather in the alley behind our homes and the trading would begin. It was then that I realized that there were *levels* of cooking prowess and some of the ladies were there primarily in hopes of "upgrading" their hopeless culinary attempts. In other words, some mothers fared much better than those of us who brought back Alpo Helper with no hope of salvation. The kids caught on much quicker than we thought and there was a starvation rebellion of monumental proportions, resulting in more leftovers than we could manage. There was no choice but to put all remaining morsels in plastic containers, burp them responsibly and lay them to rest in the refrigerator. My only hope was my husband. He would come home tired and be so happy to have food prepared for him that he didn't notice (until the children pointed the finger at me) that he was eating what they didn't finish the evening before.

The jig was up. Leftovers became my closest friends. I would open the door each morning and before the milk was removed for cereal, I would take a mental inventory of the items "available" to me in a pinch and then take a closer look at some suspicious "movement" in a few of the containers. A few of the lids appeared askew and I swear I could hear a hissing noise from a few of them. I'd check back later, I'd promise. Then laundry, boo boos, swimming lessons, and naps would intervene and before you knew it, a trip into the refrigerator was a visit to the Alexander Fleming penicillin museum. I'd get distracted by moms who would call, complaining that their son/daughter had neglected to tell them about this or that science project due in the morning and they had just finished cleaning their kitchen for the fourth time that day. What were they to do? A quick scan of the fridge and a booming enterprise was born! Word got around and soon my kitchen was the center of every parent's dream of A+ material. My finest achievement (first place in the science fair) was an active volcano (formerly a meatloaf) given to Marvin down the street. It had morphed over the months from animal/vegetable into a mineral species of sorts and was spitting unrecognizable bits out the top. Hello . . . lava! I was a legend in the neighborhood. Now don't get me wrong. I clean out the refrigerator every now and again like on New Year's Day when the rest of the family is hip deep in the bowl games, right after the Traditional Burning of the Unpaired Socks.

I guess I'm a little surprised by the posthumous tribute to science. Taking stock of the talent I was most appreciated for during my prime, I had taken the liberty a few years ago to have my head stone pre-engraved:

1949   Julie (MAMA) Felicelli   ????
"THERE GOES THE PIZZA!"

Grandchildren

Talk about the gift that keeps on giving . . . If you have grandchildren you know exactly what I am talking about. If you don't have any, imagine a piece of chocolate cake with icing that drizzles down the sides. You begin to eat it and it never gets any smaller. In fact, the frosting just keeps on drizzling down and you finally know what it's like to have your cake and eat it, too, as the saying goes. I have always been crazy about children, no matter who they belong to. I appreciate their total honesty before they learn about tact and I am even amused at their naughty times when it is clear that they have had enough of the adult world. I was always prepared to become a grandparent while some of my friends were fighting it. "How could you stand anyone calling you Grandma? I can't think of myself as a grandma, old, white-haired, and forgetful," they would complain. They must have thought grandparenthood meant some sort of sacrifice, like giving up their youth, I guess.

I jumped on the grandma train before it stopped at the station. My son Mark was friends with a girl from work, Tina, who had a beautiful, precious baby daughter. Tina was going to college while working and needed help sometimes when class schedules interfered with the care of the baby. I offered to pitch in and before long, this sweet little cherub was part of our family and called me "Grandma." Of course, the first time she called my husband "Grandpa" you could see him melt on the spot. It gave us the opportunity to wear the title, try it on for size, and it felt pretty good. She's ten now, our Killian, and she still calls us grandparents. We still love every second of it.

When our daughter Jennifer announced that she would be a mother, we couldn't have been happier, for two reasons. One, she would give us a grandchild, and two, she would finally get the chance to see what raising a child was like. There's that time between teen and adult years when kids think they know everything and can solve any problem. They are quick to point out your every mistake and quicker to assure you that they will not make those same mistakes. Payback time was on the horizon. But, as luck would have it, we were as far from them as geographically possible and it would take a trip to Alaska to see this little one. We sent care packages throughout the pregnancy but I was limited to one trip there, hopefully coinciding with the birth. I was asked to be present in the delivery room and that was the best invitation I ever got. Expressing concerns that I might be one too many persons during the birth, my daughter told me she'd rather have me in there than the doctor or her husband. Yeow! Now, that's pressure.

I arrived in Anchorage about a week before her due date, but my daughter had been in a car accident and I couldn't wait to see for myself that all was well. While we were washing clothes and getting the nursery ready, I innocently brought up the subject of naming the baby. "Yes, mom, we'll be naming her *Robitaille* (robe-a-tie). It's French and I like it." Fully aware that I was entering the arena of hormonal havoc, I said, "Oh. I took French for six years and if my memory serves me, it loosely translates to 'dress size.' Does it have any special significance?" "No, it's the name of a hockey player for the L.A. Kings," she said with much pride. "Is he the father?" I asked, looking at her husband. "No, mom, it's just a great-sounding name. *Robitaille*. We love it." In vain, I tried to tell her that no one would ever pronounce her name correctly and she would be "Robi-Tail" to everyone who didn't know the French pronunciation. I wasn't trying to be totally ignorant. "Okay," she said, "how 'bout we shorten it to *'Taille'*? That's still pretty." Their last name added to that first name would send this poor little unborn love nugget into a lifelong sentence of teasing. It would have been a blessing had their last name been *Wagon*. Tail Wagon would have been a step up from what they were imposing on her. My acting abilities and the drama with which I described her lifetime therapy sessions and the cost to her in sanity worked finally and my daughter relented. We would not have a Robitaille or Taille. Their second choice was much more normal, Victoria Elizabeth, but she couldn't let the *Taille* thing go that easily. "Tai, T-A-I. I like it. We'll name her Tai." A quick look in the *1500 Baby Names* book under Tai was, "Thai: person from Thailand." I gave up and prayed for the little sweetheart to have very thick skin.

We went together to her last appointment and the ultrasound showed that she had a slight leak in the fluid protecting the baby. The doctor sent us straight to the hospital where she was monitored. They would take the baby the next day, no problem. Her doctor, however, had made previous plans. It was his monthly turn to fly up to the frozen tundra to administer to the Eskimos and penguins. His trusted associate would do the honors. When her husband arrived, I left them alone to spend their last evening together as a couple. They would induce her labor at six o'clock the next morning and I would return for the festivities.

I couldn't sleep, so I did what every crazy Italian grandma-to-be does: I made enough food to last until the child went to kindergarten. I did manage to doze off for an hour or so and dreamed about becoming a grandma to my daughter's daughter. I had memorized the route to the hospital, so when I took off, maneuvering over the ice and snow, I made sure I allowed lots of extra time. I was driving their new van and had no desire to put the first dent in it. One more right turn and I'd be there; less than a half a mile to grandmahood. What is that in the middle of the road, I asked myself as I hit the brakes. There, in the headlights, was the biggest moose I have ever imagined. He merely turned and looked straight at me. He reacted as if he was fully aware that he had the right of way and since he was approximately the size of the van, the problem was mine, not his. I couldn't believe it. I had looked all week, everywhere we went, hoping to catch sight of a moose. Nothing. And here was one standing in between me and my granddaughter. No way, buddy. Not today. In a cunning move, I turned off my headlights and backed up about one hundred feet. It was a four lane highway and he was across at least two of them. In the darkness, I turned off the pavement and rode the sidewalk for about two hundred feet until I was sure I was past him and he wasn't charging after me. It worked! Headlights back on, I was smug the rest of the way to the hospital, parked, and raced up the six flights of stairs to see my daughter.

Six and a half hours later she was pushing hard. The doctor instructed the father to go up and stand by her shoulder and hold her hand. He looked over to me and said, "C'mon Grandma. Step right up and let's see what this is all about." Both my daughter and son-in-law nodded and I stepped forward. It was much harder to see my daughter give birth than it was to give birth myself but I saw that beautiful little person slide out, saw her confusion at all the noise. Her color was off because the cord was around her neck and I looked to the nurses to take her as soon as the cord was cut so they could massage her. The doctor was in no hurry, but the mother in all of us females took charge and away she was swept for an oxygen boost. I took pictures of her first minutes of cleaning, weighing, just being. But I was there. It has made such a difference. I saw her first breath, heard her first whimper. She will always be my right-hand girl, by my side through thick and thin. She is the spitting image of her mother and I am stunned to see the similarities.

Two years later it was time to prepare for my second daughter's big moment. It was just after Easter in St.

Louis and, again, I was invited to be a witness. We had a big baby shower and got enough presents for triplets. This would be my first grandson and he would be Nathan Joseph, two good strong names. No need for drama here. It was odd, though, that all the furniture in my daughter's home had big, black garbage bags draped over it. My daughter said her husband had heard rumors about the water bag breaking without notice and he was taking precautions. The bed was also covered in plastic as were the kitchen chairs and car seats. I asked my daughter if he was envisioning a tsunami and it was only after the doctor assured him that we were looking at a liter, two at most, that he eased up a bit.

We had everything ready when the first signs of labor began. I advised the new father in waiting to go to sleep so he would be fresh for the upcoming marathon. He opted to play video games and fell asleep twenty minutes before we had to leave. "You're kidding, right?" was his response when we woke him. She had been journaling her labor-pain experience, chronicling the time between pains, the duration of the pains and whether they were actual pain or just pressure. A look at her entries made me laugh. "Pain with pressure," "Pressure with pain," "Pain with a lot of pressure," "Pressure with a lot of pain," were repeated over and over. We waited for a few hours, to be sure it wasn't a hoax and I drove her and the groggy one to the hospital as giant snowflakes fell all around us. It was a magical sight and I mentioned that this would be one of the last moments they'd share as "just the two of us." The baby would change things as only babies can.

Pregnant women were walking the halls as we entered, trying to get things going. My daughter was disappointed that she might be put on the walkathon, too, but she was at a perfect stage for an epidural as soon as we arrived and her nurse assured us she could put the tennis shoes away. We waited until she dozed off and then the two of us not hooked up to monitors headed for the hospital cafeteria. On our trip back to the room, I tried to assure the new dad that everything was just about perfect so far. As we turned the corner, we came upon a team of janitors just outside my daughter's room, wielding mops and using an industrial water vacuum to suck up gallons of water, coming directly from my daughter's uterus, according to her husband. The look on his face said, "I knew it. Her water broke and this is the outcome; two liters my foot." We were all relieved to learn that the bathroom directly above my daughter's room was leaking through the ceiling and it wasn't my daughter at all causing the flood.

During the last stage of labor, it seemed that the baby was in some distress, not coming down the birth canal as she pushed. Her doctor recommended using a device that would suction the baby down gently. Out of the closet came another water vacuum which the doctor began to pump after he attached the suction cup to the baby's head. As the baby came out, we realized he was face up, the reason her pushing had so little effect on her progress. At the last second, the new daddy decided to jump in and help; after the baby was delivered, what was left of her water sloshed out and he jumped back about two feet. The doctor had remained calm in his head-to-toe rain gear and held on to avert disaster. The effects of the vacuum on the baby's head were mindboggling. Instead of the sweet little round head that she had begged the doctor for, the baby was the proud owner of a temporary football head, produced by the suction of the water vac. It was long and pointed and we asked immediately if that was permanent. He assured us that all would be normal in a couple of days and we passed that info on to everyone who came to visit. Except her brother. He was one of the last to arrive and we were all fussing and oohing. He walked over to the bassinet and his girlfriend snapped what she hoped would be a proud uncle picture. The look on his face when he saw the size and shape of the head asked, "Does no one but me see the noggin on this kid? Yeow!" Of course we all laughed and gave him the short version of the story. I thanked God for letting me witness another miracle. This little guy is amazing. We are proud to announce that his head is just fine and regular sized but we think the suction stimulated his brain and he's like a little Einstein. He sends us scampering to the encyclopedia more times than not to answer the questions he has about everything.

Tai needed a sibling, she was sure of it, and we never say no to another grandchild. When we found out the baby was a girl, I was afraid to ask my daughter about the name choice. "I like the name *Maxence* (Max-awnce)." Here we go again. "Why *Maxence*?" I asked, unable to believe it was even a consideration. "I've always wanted a Jake and a Maxie so I'll call her Maxence and she'll be

Maxie." "What about *MacKenzie*? Call her Mackenzie and Maxie for short." All I could think of was that she had been hit on the head. "Remember that she has to live with it and sign her Valentines every year," I added trying to find any sense in it at all. She finally came out of the blue with "Maya" and we clapped and cheered and monogrammed everything in sight so she wouldn't change her mind. When it came time for the baby, I made a pilgrimage to Indianapolis this time and we got everything ready. The doctor kept saying she wasn't ready. His guess was at least two more weeks, so I went home to get things ready for Christmas. I'd be back in a week and we'd have a baby. Five days after I left, the call came at 5:30 a.m. "I think I feel something. Today might be the day." "I'm on my way. Hang in there." It was a four-hour trip from Detroit to Indy but I was sure I had plenty of time. I called every hour to check on her progress and one of the calls was a little more intense than I hoped. "I'll answer your question in a minute, Mom. Could you wait until I'm done with this pain?" What! She was in big-time labor and I was still an hour and a half away. "Are you dressed? Get Tai and be ready in five minutes. I'll call Mrs. G and she'll come and get you. I'll take the shortcut and meet you at the hospital." Just then Mother Nature sent a full-blown blizzard. I called my friend to ask her to get to my daughter as fast as she could and drive her for me, and she was on the case. This was about 9:45 in the morning. At 10:20 I got the call that they barely made it to a hospital ten minutes from the house, not the intended hospital an hour away. The baby was born on the emergency room table at 10:12, less than six minutes after arriving. I missed it. I missed it. I missed it. I couldn't get over that. It happened without me. The snowstorm was savage and it took twice as long to make the rest of the trip but it was all over. When I got there, Maya was the talk of the town — the Emergency Room Baby. No one could believe how this woman was having a baby in the parking lot. She couldn't get out of the car and they barely got her in the wheelchair and into the room before the baby came flying out. Everything was fine but no one had seen anything like this before; my granddaughter, the Emergency Room Baby, and my daughter, the lady in the parking lot. All this hubbub and I missed it. She was already hooked up for her hearing test when I saw her for the first time. I kissed my daughter, told her how beautiful Maya was, and then went to look for my friend, who drove her here and was probably shaking in her boots after the experience. She was sitting with Tai, coloring in a book as if nothing traumatic happened. Tai was excited and bewildered but my friend was waiting for the opportunity to crumple. She would never have signed up for this job, if given the choice. Friends are friends for a reason. I expected her to whack me for putting her in the position of possibly delivering a baby on the roadside. It was hair-raising, I'll give you that. Instead, she went home and took a nap. Maybe had a glass of wine, and put her feet up. I actually envied her. She got the first look at this grandchild. She would admit it changed her life. I know the feeling. It will be a few years before her daughter makes her a grandma. It will be hard to top this day in excitement but she'll know just what to do. It comes with the territory.

Maya has a great sense of humor and an unbelievably darling disposition. She probably figures she already caused enough commotion on her entry into the world. She can take it easy for awhile. And come see Grandma as often as she can. Oh, and bring the others, too. There's always room for grandchildren.

Clean It Up

The cleaning crew will be here any minute. It's nearly 8:30 in the morning and I have been up for almost three hours getting ready. You hear about those people who clean the house before the cleaning people get there. Trust me. I am NOT one of those people. It took thirty-three years to get my husband to agree to let someone come in to do bathrooms, dusting and vacuuming. It was the best day of my life. The swat team arrived on time and took off into corners I hadn't noticed in decades. They had machines that sucked up the big stuff and ones that skirted the base boards to get the pesky flora and fauna that took up residence there. It was magical. I laid out cookies, water and soda in a buffet spread on the counter and ran upstairs to see if I had any leftover chiffon dresses. I pictured myself coming down the stairs as my husband returned after a hard day's work, me swathed in layers and layers of softness, smiling sweetly, his slippers in my hand. We would discuss the day's events and make plans for the future. We would see our images reflected in all the bright and shiny newly polished fixtures.

That dream faded when I caught a glimpse of a crew member and she looked like a deer in the headlights. "There's a strange noise coming from the blue bedroom." Without a moment's hesitation I replied, "Oh, that's our teenager's room. He's buried under one of the piles. He probably fell asleep on his remote control car and it's the low battery warning. Also there might be something else living up there. All our pets are accounted for but something is attacking his socks in the hamper. Just do your best. Thanks." The next girl I bump into is running out of our daughter's room, panic-stricken and screaming, "There's an attack cat in there! It jumped out from under the bed and came at me with paws flailing, hissing like crazy!" It was Mariah, our daughter's nine-year-old cat. I tell her, "She has no front claws, so that's all show. She likes Harry Connick Jr. so let me put a tape in for her and she should be fine. She'll go back under the bed and enjoy the music. Just to be sure, though, don't turn your back on her when you are vacuuming."

We have a two-story home and a basement, so there is activity on three floors at once. I am just calming down from the cat incident when I hear another scream, this one water related. Taking two stairs at a time (no small feat for these stumpy legs), I run straight into another of the girls, sopping wet from head to toe. "You tried to turn on the shower, didn't you? It took a trip to the hardware store for us to see how that contraption works. You didn't pull that knob, did you? Well, that's the problem right there." It seems the genius who designed this shower unit thought it was a great idea to place a ring on the faucet that you must bend down to pull in order for the shower to operate. And, to work the hand-held unit, you have to pull a knob on top of the unit hard but not too hard.

My husband and I found out the hard way. We had been in the house a week and it was time for our son to break down and take a shower. We heard the water running for a half hour and had visions of a soapy, shampoo-riddled pre-teen, who smelled winter fresh. Not so. He called for help and we both entered to see our son, naked, struggling to get any of it operational. "Don't pull that thing," I warned my husband. "I tried that yesterday and water came flying out like a fire hydrant. I'm not kidding." I always have to add that because for some reason my husband suspects that I am always kidding and he never takes my warnings seriously. As usual, he paid no attention and pulled the button, and hard. Our son, sitting on the commode, looking a lot like Rodin's *Thinker*, watched in horror as a spout of water at least three inches in diameter attacked his father and me, drenching us totally. It was one of those times when you had to laugh or injure an internal organ holding it back. We laughed because we were wet and he was naked, and he laughed to see his two parents so humbled, looking like drowned mops. It was one of the best family moments we have had in some time. And to further the fun, our son begged us not to give the hint to his unsuspecting siblings when they visited. Each came down, wrapped in a towel, asking for the secret to the shower dilemma. It was a chance for *him* to teach *them* a little something for a change. Our soaking wet houseguest was only mildly interested in the whole story, so we gave her some dry clothing to change into and threw her wet mess into the dryer.

It was almost 3:00, and there were no signs of them. I put food out for lunch and it had disappeared so I hoped they had the strength to survive. I was actually hiding now, knowing they were giving each other the "eye" like, "Holy Smokes, it's a never-ending battle here." Exactly. If I had to describe my predicament it would be to picture a dog, head barely above water, paddling like crazy and getting nowhere. Try thirty years of that feeling. This was my chance to reach shore, to move on to something, any-thing, else. These girls were my ticket out, and I wasn't going to ruin it. I even let them play country music that day and I hate country music. It sounds too much like whining kids.

I must have yelled "You're grounded" at the radio a few too many times because the girls offered to let me change the station. They probably averted a violent act. When they staggered out at 3:30, there was little left of the starch they showed earlier. I thanked them, told them I loved them, and offered to let them rifle through my drawers in case there was a memento they would like to have to remember the day. I don't think they heard me because they were knocking each other over to get out of the house and down the stairs to the car. They'll be back, I said, trying to console myself. A walk through the house brought tears to my eyes as I noticed things buried just this morning, like my son. It lasted a few hours that day — the euphoria. Then the kids came home and someone thought it was a good idea to let the dogs out of the kennel for a try inside the house. I called my husband to come home immediately if he wanted any chance of seeing the house in its new condition. He tried, but traffic was a mess and he made it just in time to see the dogs leap on my chiffon dress with muddy paws and knock me down the stairs.

As I was tumbling down, I told him how great it looked before the kids and the dogs. "You're kidding, right?" he said and I knew he'd never believe me.

I never saw that first group again. Someone said one of them quit, one moved to a third-world country, and another thought she'd give dental assistant school a second chance. I've had several teams come and go and the duo I have now are tough and come armed and pre-pared. I try to meet them part of the way on Tuesday mornings. There are a few housekeeping commandments I adhere to: (1) Thou shalt take the 457 floating toys out of the Jacuzzi, left by the grandchildren as they sent every-thing sailing across the tub via the jet stream. (2) Thou shalt chip everything chippable from under the kitchen table. And, the greatest of all, (3) Thou shalt not come upon anyone's shed underwear unexpectedly. It's the least I can do before they get here. And while I'm at it, I throw a load in the dishwasher, empty the trash, do a few loads of laundry. I am NOT cleaning before they come — I'm cleaning so they WILL come. There is a difference.

Prank

*O*ur family doesn't have the budget that the TV "Gotcha" shows have but with this large family we have pulled off some doozies in the prank department. Our last one didn't even start off as a prank and came in under ten dollars. We had been planning a special birthday party for my friend Mary's seven-year-old granddaughter for three months and we were coming to the final preparations with one big hurdle ahead. We needed a super duper cake to go with the theme—a garden tea party. Many friends had joined forces to make this party spectacular. My California friend, Chris, had designed and made dozens of little dresses for the attendees and a spectacular petal-layered one for the birthday girl that made her look like a fairy princess. We decorated garden hats, filled party bags, invented games, and stuffed a teapot piñata to the brim with goodies. This was going to be the party to end all parties. The cake had to be extra special. Our first thought was to make it in the shape of a teapot but it needed to travel with us three hundred miles and we could just picture the spout and handle breaking away from the main cake during the trip, so we looked for a suitable substitute. Finding a twelve-inch daisy cake pan, we thought we had it made with a cute flower cake. We bought frosting and cake-decorating sugars and sprinkles. We were pumped. My younger daughter Annie was especially excited about it and drew designs so we would know exactly how she thought it should look. While she was at work, her sister, Emily, and I would bake, frost, and decorate this floral delicacy and it would be ready for the trip when Annie came home from work.

We followed the directions, greasing and flouring the pans, everything according to the box. The pans were bigger than a usual round cake so we used one extra mix and poured half into each pan. It took longer to cook than usual and when the pans came out of the oven, everything looked great. We let them cool for a few minutes and began the process of loosening them. We edged the rims with a knife, turned them over to tap them out but they didn't budge. The major portion of the cake was stuck. Repeated attempts to extract it were unsuccessful and we ended up taking it out in pieces, none of them equal. We prayed to the frosting gods and hoped we could piece it together but there were some chasms that even frosting could not disguise. Everything else for the party was so spectacular. We couldn't let this spoil our perfect party plan. A quick call to the bakery with specific directions for what we needed, and the cake problem was solved. We would pick it up when we got to the party the next day.

There sat this big, ugly, uneven confection with frosting three inches thick in some areas keeping it together, and it was Emily's diabolical side that suggested we scheme to play a trick on her sister. We would decorate it as if we were bringing it with us for the party and to top it off, the schemer would inform this poor unsuspecting creature that she would have to carry it on her lap all the way because the car was stuffed with party items. When Annie called home to see how things were going, Emily shared with her that while I was resting, she went ahead and decorated the cake for me. She went on about how she had outlined the petals, inscribed it with another color and had even used sanding sugars in the center to resemble pollen, just to make it more realistic. I was listening on the line and could barely conceal my hysteria.

The outlining of the petals was irregular at best and the pollen was a clump of coagulated sugar, but it was the inscription that literally took the cake. Emily used red for the outline, green for the letters, and used a hyphen after "birth" and put "day" on the next line. For the child's name, she put one letter to the left of the largest crevice and the remaining three letters to the right. It was hideous, her best work ever. The cake was still a little warm, so the frosting began to sag, lengthening the lettering to a pitiful size and shape. We could hardly look at it without recoiling in horror and we had to practice remaining calm, so we would be ready for our award performances.

As planned, I was alone in the kitchen when our "mark" caught her first glimpse of the cake. "Mom . . . what happened?" she asked and I replied, "She tried so hard. She knew I was tired and wanted to help. Look. She even put pollen in the center for authenticity. She really worked hard."

"But Mom . . . everything else is so perfect. We can't take that cake to the party. It's awful. It will ruin everything we planned. Think of the birthday girl."

"Do you want to tell your sister that her donation to the party is unacceptable? She was so proud of her work. You know how shy she is. It really took a lot for her to do this. Oh, by the way, you'll have to carry it on your lap. We don't have any flat space left in the car."

"Mom, no. We can't use that cake. It will spoil everything. The dress, hats, jewelry . . . everything else is spectacular. We can't bring that cake."

"Okay, go get your sister and you'll have to tell her. And remember, she's only been off Prozac for a few days." Just then, the cake fraud walked in innocently to take credit and get glory for her efforts. We tried not to look at each other but as soon as our eyes met, we started to laugh, not the out loud kind, but the silent, belly shaking laugh. We couldn't get control of ourselves and after what seemed like forever, Annie noticed our faces and she was so mad that we would fake her out like this. She couldn't believe our cruelty and promised revenge. At the same time, she was so relieved that this cake would not make the trip. We took pictures of it, just before one of the crevices collapsed and sent a river of frosting cascading across the table. We left for the party before dinner, but the story circulating around the house is that our son videotaped the remainder of the disaster and took it to school for extra credit. They were learning about the awful effects of mudslides. He only got four out of five extra points because she didn't understand his choice of colors and she couldn't figure out what the awful yellow stuff was. We didn't tell Emily. We'd hate to crush her creative side. The pollen was a stroke of genius.

Let's All Vent Our Spleens
(It's Almost Over, I Promise)

Concerts

Been to a concert lately? Or a sporting event or any public place that seats more than five thousand people? I'll admit it's been a few years, but the scars remain and it would take a miracle of great proportions to get me to attend any future event. I'm the first to admit I've not kept up with behavior trends, but I had savored such high hopes of fun and entertainment with our entire family. I only bit the inside of one cheek as I purchased ten tickets for roughly the price I paid for my first car. It would be fun, I told myself, to have all of us assembled, paying homage to the one and only Paul Simon. I was equally interested in seeing the sidekick performance of Bob Dylan in hopes they'd have a screen with lyrics so I could finally figure out what he was singing about and have some closure to my confusion in the sixties. Our seats were in the first section so we could leave our binoculars at home. *Our seats.* We paid for seats. Okay, we probably rented them for the evening if you want to get picky, but there are letters and numbers on the seats and you have to go there when you enter the amphitheatre and silly me, I thought the money would guarantee that you could actually sit in them.

Enter alcoholic beverages. On our way in from the parking lot, there were souvenir, food, and beverage stands lining both sides of the venue. There was a smattering of customers getting a program (for approximately the cost of a root canal), a few getting hot dogs and popcorn (for the price of four new radial tires), and then there was the beer line. It twisted and curved for as far as the eye could see and the management happily provided a shuttle bus to move people from their seat section to the back of the beer line in the parking lot. Of course, this concession stand opened hours before the show and by the time the performance began, you could see what havoc the frothy beverage had wrought on misguided music lovers. To warm up the crowd, the Macarena blared over the speakers, and it was the middle age moms who got most excited. It was apparent they had practiced secretly at home and had mastered the diverse arm movements. It seemed extremely important to them to show the other concert goers that they were hip and time was not passing them by. The alcohol, however, made the quarter turn a little tricky, and many mothers and their drinks landed on the people and seats nearby. I'm no scientist and I am not familiar with the time it takes alcohol to have its way with the brain before settling in the bladder but you'd think people would take care of that before curtain time. As Paul Simon walked on stage to begin the show, the whole row in front of us stood up as the weakest bladder owner crawled clumsily over the others to take care of the dilemma. Maybe they should have a *Depend's* concession stand. We had all rearranged our seats so that the shortest kids were not sitting behind the biggest heads but there's not much you can do with a person whose hair, in the throes of humidity, looks like mutant cotton candy. And it didn't help that her nose put Cyrano de Bergerac's beak to shame. We were so transfixed that we almost forgot Paul Simon. Then there was the drunk (whose hearing was temporarily impaired and could not seem to find where he was sitting) who thought he could sing along with both performers when he apparently knew none of the words.

There are the lawn seats, after all, for people who must dance and show off their skills in public. Indignant, we asked the ushers if they could help. They asked the perpetrators politely, once, and then disappeared for the remainder of the show. We never actually saw Paul Simon or Bob Dylan that night. Both the stage and the big screens were covered by the flailing bodies and appendages surrounding us. I still don't know what Bob Dylan was singing. And I actually envied the hearing impaired who had someone signing the words for them. The mystery was solved for them but to this day I am clueless. And if there were any people sitting down, Paul Simon, in some delusional moment, invited everyone to their feet. That's when I gave up. I'm old, yes. I expect to sit in a seat I pay for, yes. I expect people to control their behavior in a public place, yes. Great expectations, little gratification. I love music, all types, but I draw the line at sifting through thousands of mini dramas as I listen in public. My husband saved my musical sanity when he came home with the ultimately perfect gift. He had left the house one Saturday on the salami/bread run that was his habit. It is a well-known fact that his wallet has hinges and it needs oiling regularly for lack of use. So, imagine my surprise when he comes home with a grandfather clock, new kitchen table and chairs set, a fifty-five-inch TV, and a grand piano that plays by itself. I figured he had suffered a stroke in the salami line and did not realize that these items cost money, lots of money, but he was hooked when he heard the piano play and bought the other items while he was under the influence of Liberace. We are now the proud parents of several wonderful tapes that have live piano music and a stereo that accompanies the piano with vocals and instrumentation. Guess who's in my living room this morning? Josh Grobin, Barry Manilow, Billy Joel, Michael Bolton, and yes, even Paul Simon. I can have them entertain me any time I want. Okay, I don't actually see them but that's no different from going to a concert now, is it? And if I do get the urge to share some musical entertainment in the presence of other humans, I head straight for the symphony. Get this. No one stands up during the performance. Drinks are not allowed into the auditorium. They don't play the Macarena before the performance begins. You don't step on any peanuts or get gum stuck to the bottom of your shoes. Comments are held until the applause. No underwear is thrown into the string section. The rudest behavior is excusable as the comfortable seating usually takes a toll on a few who doze off and actually snore. The percussion section usually drowns them out, and at peak moments wakes them up, all to our great entertainment.

Now, there is little you or anyone can do to convince me that it would be worth the trouble and inconvenience of facing another massive gathering. I'd probably risk opening old wounds for the Pope and if I'm being totally honest, there is one other unique personality that still intrigues me, even at my advanced age. My kids have listened to him nonstop for years and I tell you, he's one clever entertainer, however eclectic. I have to imagine that his concerts start out in an unusual fashion, and for the several costume changes he must make, you are transported anywhere and everywhere you want to go. My kids have attended in several cities and said it was, by far, the best entertainment for the buck. Anyone know where Weird Al Yankovic is playing these days? I especially appreciated his take on Michael Jackson's *Beat It* with *Eat It*. I love food songs. *I Lost On Jeopardy* still gets me, too. And that new hardware song is the theme my husband plays while he's on his errands most Saturdays. We don't let him go anywhere alone anymore. One more impulse purchase and we'll have to move to a bigger house.

Road Rage

Reports of road rage incidents always shock me. How could any one person get so mad at another person or another person's vehicle that he would actually resort to using a weapon or running the person and the vehicle off the road? Does anyone think that he or she owns the road and others do not have permission to use it or that everyone should pull over until they are finished? Evidently so, according to statistics. Road rage is up and tolerance is at an all-time low. Every day you encounter people who should not be behind the wheel of a grocery cart, let alone several tons of steel. They seem to have forgotten everything they ever learned in driver's ed, and only use the *Rules Of The Road* book to level the pool table legs.

Now, here is where it gets complicated. Persons with far too much free time on their hands have decided that there are levels of driving problems. They contend that road rage is a totally separate thing from aggressive driving. And aggressive driving is totally different from just plain, old bad driving. When it's happening to you, your emotions don't have those distinctions in mind. You are most often driving at high speeds when some nincompoopish miscreant decides he would like to use the part of the road that you are presently occupying. His turn signal, if used at all, is applied at least ten seconds after he has run you off the road. The look in his eye tells you that you are not the first or last person who has interrupted his need to own and control the road. He weaves in and out of lanes and swerves onto the shoulder if he can get in front of you faster. He's going at least twenty miles an hour faster than you and he doesn't seem to notice that both of you come to the stop light at exactly the same time, despite his efforts to clear the roads for his personal satisfaction. And there's actually a driver worse than this that doesn't deserve the space on paper to even mention. He's the motorcycle rider who believes he has the right to pass in between you and the car riding next to you, subjecting himself to the possibility of becoming the creamy filling of an auto sandwich cookie.

My kids would tell you that I'm loaded with road rage. At stop signs I carry on one-sided conversations, urging people to remember that they are in a moving vehicle, and that after a three-second pause, it is their right and duty to proceed in a safe manner through the intersection. My mother believes firmly that you must wait until all traffic from the other three ways has disappeared before it is safe to go. She gets many honks and even more one-finger waves from the crowd building behind her but she remains firm in this belief. It is evident that there are many people who share her belief and if I'm stuck at a stop sign more than a minute and a half, I will admit that I begin speaking in tongues. "What's the holdup here? This is not the time to readjust your floor mats, or read your auto manual. C'mon, people, it's not a rest stop. Let's keep moving." It relieves tension and appears to help traffic, too. My children act as if I am ramming into the back of a car that did not take off fast enough. "Mother, calm down," they say as if I am angry. I'm merely mentioning things that should be apparent to all who drive. I happily inform them that the definition of traffic is "the passage of people or vehicles along routes of transportation." The key here is "passage" and "routes of transportation." Those words imply movement and that is all I am asking for. I have kept anger out of it. If I become vexed, I usually pretend that the car in front of me is being driven by a little old man whose wife is pointing out every flower, every cute child, and every sweet little puppy. If he doesn't slow down and pretend to look he will hear about it to his dying day. And that game has worked fairly well — until today. Today, I was pushed beyond my limits and I must admit that acts of violence on anther person and his or her vehicle came to mind.

There's a spiffy shortcut from our home to our son's high school and it saves me about ten minutes from the regular route. His calls are always the same. He has usually forgotten something or is in need of money ASAP. I chastise him for being too forgetful and for interrupting my action-packed day but after the grumbling I make the four-mile trip within a reasonable length of time. On this particular occasion, I noticed that the car in front of me, a luxury SUV, was moving at a snail's pace and the driver was making unusual hand gestures. He was using his left hand to speak on a cell phone but he was plucking something from the seat beside him and inspecting his choice. He must be a diamond salesman and he's describing different stones to the caller on the other end as he picks them up. Still, he only has two hands which leaves him two short for the steering wheel. Oh, now he's placed the object in his mouth. Yech! From his side mirror I could tell that my little old man theory would not apply in this instance. Dark hair and swarthy eyebrows were looking back at me and unless his passengers were bound and gagged in the back, he was traveling alone. Again, he picked up an item from the next seat, looked at it carefully and popped it into his mouth. By this time the flavor must have gotten to him and he slowed down to fifteen miles per hour in a twenty-five zone. I don't know if I was angrier about the slow speed or the fact that he was driving with no hands. At any rate, I contemplated jumping out of my car, catching up with him, pulling him out and shaking him to his senses. Don't you know my son is fifty cents short of lunch money, you fool? Lunch period is only twenty minutes long and he will be hungry. He won't be able to concentrate and he won't pass History and now he won't graduate. Thanks a lot, mister. Taking my short, stocky legs into account, I decided on a less daring move. I pulled around him at my first opportunity, thoughts of my poor son living at home more years than necessary spurring me on. From my own less luxurious SUV I peered into the passenger seat to see what was so enticing. The man was snacking from a relish tray the size of my dining room table! There were stuffed olives, carved radishes, curvy carrot sticks, celery stalks, artichoke hearts and more. Plus dip. He had it all. Right there next to him, for his munching convenience. His wife was so thoughtful. No, I'll bet it was his mother. Nobody under fifty makes the flower radishes anymore. His wife probably told him the kitchen was closed. He could pick something up on the way. A quick stop at Mom's and his little tummy was all better now, wasn't it? Well, I gave him "the look" as I passed. He probably doesn't know how close he came to being dragged and beaten beyond recognition by a grandma. It took a while but I calmed down and came up with a plan.

Everyone says you shouldn't hold things in. You should express yourself, get things off your chest, and not keep anything bottled up. It's hard to do while driving but I found something that just might work. I located a company that makes those electronic message boards and they are about the perfect size to fit into the back window of most cars. They send a running scroll of information across the screen and do it in pretty quick order. Now I can hear you critics saying, "Yeah, now she'll be the one driving with no hands. What's the difference between her and the next idiot?" Good question. Everything but refrigerators are voice activated these days. Why can't we have a voice-activated info board that would express our concerns to cars approaching us? Something like "Don't forget that interval, pal. One car length for every ten miles. Thanks and have a nice day," or "Don't forget— your turn signal is your friend. I can't read your mind, buddy." Imagine when you are part of a caravan of cars and no one can get a cell phone to work and several bladders in your vehicle are about to blow. What better way to communicate than sending the message: "Tinkle alert! It's the next rest stop or I'll need that case of paper towels we packed in the trailer. This is not a joke, I repeat, this is not a joke." And you can press the repeat button to run it as long as necessary. I bought the convenient six-pack and put one in the back window, one in each side window (for those unexpected lane changing fools) one custom made to read backwards for the jerk who eventually glances in his rear-view mirror, and a revolving one for the top of my SUV that rotates by satellite feed for any occasion. In stop-and-go traffic they make perfect sense. Pass on condolences as you wait for the funeral procession to pass by. "I am so sorry for your loss," or informational, "Lady you forgot your child at checkout lane number three. Please return to the grocery store to claim him," are only a few of the limitless possibilities. The last one I saved for my bike. I don't have to worry about rude drivers anymore. The same scroll runs constantly with, "Honk and I will memorize your license plate, find out where you live, and make your life a living hell." It works great. Just make sure you turn off the voice activation before you sing along with your favorite song on the radio. You wouldn't want just anyone knowing you don't really know the words to any of the latest hits.

Pet Peeve

Each morning as the sun rises, I take the time to look out at nature unfolding around me. I hear the birds chirping, see the squirrels scurrying, watch the sky lighting up, and I look heavenward to say thanks for the beauty and to compliment the Creator for a job spectacularly done. It's a great day to walk and the sooner the better. No excuses today. Neighbors marvel as I spring from the house, ready to carpe the diem. My first task is to get out of the subdivision before anyone stops my flow, wanting to "chat." Once clear of familiar houses, I take on the guise of a foreign person who doesn't understand English. I just smile so I can get my heart rate, or sweat glands, or something or other activated. Life is fabulous, everything is possible and then, from around the corner comes the sighting that reduces me to the fetal position instantly, turns me into a mumbling lunatic, and takes all the starch out of my plans for the rest of the day. I can hardly put the words down, it has such a devastating effect on me. Okay, here goes.

A person is walking towards me, pet in tow, and while I know I should recognize her beautiful smile, trim thighs or fashionable shoes, I find myself fixated on the grossest sight imaginable. In her left hand is the dog leash, wrapped several times around her wrist for control of her pet. But in her right hand, for reasons I cannot understand, is a clear bag filled with (excuse me while I gag) DOG POOP! She is swinging it like it's a bouquet of flowers and it's dog poop! The bag is swelling with the stuff and while I do recognize the responsibility she accepts in cleaning up after her pet, come on . . . she's probably on a three-mile course with her precious eighty-pound Trixie (the name of whom I learned as she struggled to remove its teeth from my ankle). I'm sorry, but even in the best of circumstances that bag has to be stinking like the elephant house at the zoo by the time she gets home. Does she use only one bag for the whole trip? Please tell me she doesn't keep opening the same one to make deposits as Trixie spreads her wealth around the neighborhood. If it gets too heavy and breaks, does she have a claim with the newspaper boy for delivering her paper in inferior bags? Can she request that her newspapers be delivered in specific colored bags so they go with the dog's neck scarf, or worse, with the outfit she's wearing? I've seen yellow, pink, blue, and orange bags and I've got to tell you, poop looks like poop in every color bag! Correct me if I'm wrong, but they are, for the most part, see-through! Even in a brown paper bag, the shape is unmistakable!

And if that isn't bad enough, there are diabolical pet owners that pretend to be responsible. Yes! I passed a goodie two-shoes type swinging her bag proudly, yet never bent over to pick up the artwork created by her pooch. I thought I had noticed black marks evenly distributed across the contents of her bag (remember, I'm fixated on this) and with a slap to my forehead a la Colombo, it hit me: she was toting a few leftover bratwursts from the weekend cookout! She had no intention of picking up poop. I wouldn't be surprised if she did this on a regular basis and carried a few brats in her pocket to "fill" the bag as needed. Oh yes, people, it gets worse. If you think about it, there are probably skin flints that use the same bag for days ("Buffy poops less than our hamster") and where do they store that thing? I don't want to know but I must find out. It's so devastating to my well-being that I'm thinking of starting my own campaign, first in our town, then expanding nationwide. We'll build receptacles and call them "Doodle Dumpsters" and design them in the shape of trees or fire hydrants. Once the doodle is deposited, a burst of fresh air will be emitted into the nostrils of the pet owner and a flattened corrugated box will slip out of a slot for the next use. It will be a plastic-lined container with a mini air freshener attached, and, with a few twists, will resemble a bakery box. The dumpster will be maintained like the bathroom of a fancy hotel by persons whose salaries will rival that of the U.S. president. It's worth it, people. A day without the tell-tale swinging bag, no matter what color, will pay for itself in sanity in no time. Write letters to your congressmen, let's get this going. Moms, sponsor bake sales. Dads, clean out the garage and have yard sales. Kids, sell lemonade or cheese. Send your donations to the National Organization Prohibiting Ostentatious & Obvious Poophandling By Annoying Good Samaritans (NO POOP BAGS), don't delay. The gag reflex you save may be your own.

Tissue Tactics

How hard is it to change a toilet paper roll? Really? I'm thinking I must be a genius because I have got it down to five seconds a roll change and no one else in this house appears to have mastered or attempted to try this tricky but necessary household obligation. Panic sets in when the red lines appear on the end of the roll, signaling the need for the change. Now, you're probably asking yourself, where do I buy toilet paper with red lines at the end? I'm sorry to tell you that they don't sell it anywhere. I unwrap each roll and hand paint those lines on. Yes. The last twenty-foot section is clearly marked with perfect striations to signal that, soon, very soon depending on the condition of your digestive system, you will need to remove that little cardboard cylinder and replace it with a new, cushiony, full cylinder of, if you're lucky, at least two-ply tissue. Now I find it helpful, giving a warning that a change is impending. There is ample time to prepare and in the worst-case scenario, the pressure of such a change might be helpful to release some pent-up problems, if you get my drift. So what's the problem?

Visit any one of my six bathrooms. (Six, count them, six. After years of waiting in line for a turn, we had bathrooms built with a kitchen and a few bedrooms attached. We added a roof and a garage as afterthoughts but we had what we needed.) Anyhow, if you're on the bathroom tour, which I only take if I hear suspicious water-related noises, you will see a phenomenon that has baffled scientists and haunted mothers since the beginning of time. There will be an empty roll on the spindle with relatives strewn all over the floor, dozens of them. Does the roll reproduce itself in the night, you ask? Is there a moment when the cardboard has a need to send spores out into the universe that turn into baby rolls? They appear to be the exact size as the one on the roll. Is that the king roll? Is it necessary that it have other rolls to rule? I just don't get it.

I could understand the problem if there was something special about the cardboard. There are no words of wisdom to read, no fortune, not even your lucky numbers anywhere, outside or inside. I've looked. I have pored over this issue many times while I have been hiding from my children, looking for a peaceful moment. I have held symposiums at local VFWs in hopes of eradicating this country-wide problem. During the question-and-answer period, my heart breaks to see the faces of mothers who have given up trying, who can't remember a single time when they have finally gotten their turn in the bathroom and haven't seen that last little shred hanging limp. And while we are wiping tears of sympathy, I give them the good news. There is hope. I have developed a program, and have devised helpful hints.

First, make everyone aware of the lifesaving invention of toilet paper by reviewing its history. Get out snacks, make popcorn, because you are in for some fun. It is rumored that, originally, toilet paper was used in China in 875 A.D. It was probably made of papyrus or bamboo or something scratchy and Marco Polo brought back spaghetti instead so it probably wasn't that impressive, or maybe it was too impressive. Early in this country, leaves, mail-order catalogs and (no thank you very much) corn cobs were employed for the purpose of absorption and hygiene. No wonder no one was ever smiling in those photos of old. Rashes and itching were probably everyday occurrences. We didn't see real toilet paper until 1857, when Joseph Gayetty came out with flat sheets, and surprisingly enough, they didn't catch on. Sears had the audacity to print colored catalogues by this time and the wax-paper gloss was anything but helpful. Plus, because the pages were not colorfast, it was difficult to explain why your backside was sporting the heavy tools section. Are we having fun yet? We're coming to the climax now. Enter the Scott Brothers: Thomas, Edward, and Clarence. A whole decade after Gayetty, this Philadelphia trio got to the seat of the problem and sold small perforated rolls from push carts. Well, were you going to be the only one on the block without your own personal supply? How do you borrow a few sheets of you-know-what along with a cup of sugar? No, now there was social pressure to keep up with Joneses, Smiths, and O'Callahans. The brothers were forced to start the Scott Paper Company, in existence today because we have not found the cure for the elimination process. And one final light note, to bring even the toughest cynic to his knees. There was the Great 1973 TP Shortage, started by none other than the late Johnny Carson. He jokingly mentioned a rumor that toilet paper was in danger of becoming scarce (a layoff at logging camps, perhaps?) Shelves were cleared in days and when he tried to convince people that it was just a joke, their teeny little minds assumed he had been paid to cover up the shortage crisis and not a roll could be found for weeks. Thank God eBay wasn't invented yet. Phew. History lesson complete.

Now let's dissect the problem. Is it the roll itself that presents the problem or is it some diabolical plot by devious spindle makers? When you try to push one side toward the center to remove the dowel, the spring leaps into canon action, and like a heat-seeking missile, heads straight for the toilet where you have most probably just finished your business. Many a person has flushed the whole shebang down rather than fish out the errant spring. I'll have a remedy for that later, I promise. For now, though, let's hold a cardboard roll in each hand. There's plenty for everyone. Lightweight, they serve many useful purposes. Can anyone name something we could do with them? I hear some grunting from the back. Shove them up what? The group, getting into the spirit, rolls across the floor laughing. Good, you have the right attitude. With about a yard of dental floss you can string five or six freshly painted ones together to make a colorful necklace for Grandma's birthday? I can see you. I'm looking through my spyglass and I see you whacking your brother with an empty roll. You are so creative. There's no end to the fun but we promised a solution for the spindle problem so let's tackle that next.

The whole "seat up, seat down" problem is a real culprit here. The seat should always be DOWN, case closed, especially when handling this precarious situation. You automatically head straight for the commode and rarely notice that the last person left you in the lurch. Great if you're coming in and the urge isn't pressing, not so much if you've waited until the final commercial break to relieve yourself. Do NOT get up if you run short of paper during the process. Use tools like the toilet bowl brush or plunger to open the cabinet and poke at the package until a roll falls out. Call in little children to assist you but do NOT stand up. Show the spindle who's in charge here. Squeeze, release. Take it off the holder firmly. Squeeze, release. Not your cheeks, the spindle, silly. You're in control. If it's too far for you to reach from a sitting position, call a handyman (AFTER you've replaced the spindle) and have the holder moved to within your reach ASAP. When you are comfortable with the spindle mechanism, gently slip on the new roll, right side to left (I'm making this part up, no letters lefties) and again, squeeze, release, squeeze, release as you slip one end in the hangar and then the other side. Release. Done. Don't be surprised if you have a euphoric sensation for the first couple of times. It's normal. Your adrenaline has been waiting a long time to kick in for this.

For you weak-of-heart types and those confused types who have not laid down the law about the toilet seat remaining in the DOWN position, or who like to live on the edge by standing while performing this delicate maneuver, you will need the following supplies: a fish or butterfly net, the longest barbecue tongs you can find, a barf bag if you're the queasy type and lots and lots of hot sudsy water. Most important of all is safety glasses. You don't want to begin to explain how you put an eye out during your short stay in the bathroom.

My friends have called to tell me that the problem has been solved already and I am too late with my goodie two-shoes hints. It seems quadruple rolls are on market shelves today, complete with handy new spindles that protrude into your personal space forcing your legs to push the roll back towards the wall to sit down. For decades, happy crochet addicts have fashioned dolls and hats to cover toilet paper, to keep it discreetly hidden until needed. So now there's one more thing coming out of the closet. Next, they'll be selling the little lights like they put over impressive artwork. You wouldn't want to miss seeing that massive wad taunting you. It's not a solution, though. It just puts off the inevitable. Has anyone gotten to the bottom of a roll yet? What does it look like? If they were smart they'd put a thought for the day or a good joke or something. What's the average length of time one roll lasts if you use four sheets per time, you have 2.3 children, and you serve no beans at mealtime? You could always buy two of the monster rolls, install them on either side of the toilet and push out, relax, push out, relax. Voila. You can work on your thighs while you're sitting there. And so you don't think I'm a know-it-all, we finally had to install electronic devices that works like smoke detectors. You hear a warning bell at the one-half-roll mark, a series of bell rings at the one-quarter mark and when it gets down to the last few pieces, a shrill buzzer sounds and we can all run in to find out who the perpetrator is. We sometimes miss the offender but we can always find them. They're the ones with that little piece of toilet paper stuck to the bottom of their shoes.

About the Author

Julie Fairfield Felicelli's number has finally come up; one husband, seven children, and four grand-children make her thirteenth on the list. Fifty-six years of living, loving, and laughing and she is ready to let a little of it spill out of her and into the lives of others. It's not that she finally got everything right and felt the urge to pass it on. It's more like she tossed in the towel, admitted that per-fection, or near perfection, is unattainable, and finally admitted that life is pretty entertaining when you don't take it too seriously.

From her beginnings in Barrington, IL in 1949, she has moved many times and has celebrated many new begin-nings. Each city she lived in brought new experiences, new friends, and an appreciation of how much she had when she took the time to look and laugh. Volunteering in every city in which she has lived has allowed her to leave something behind, while moving on.